The People Management Clinic

Answers to Your Most Frequently Asked Questions

Martin Richardson

Viva Books
New Delhi | Mumbai | Chennai | Kolkata
Bengaluru | Hyderabad | Kochi | Guwahati

First Indian Edition 2012

VIVA BOOKS PRIVATE LIMITED

- 4737/23 Ansari Road, Daryaganj, New Delhi 110 002
  E-mail: vivadelhi@vivagroupindia.net, Tel. 42242200
- 76, Service Industries, Shirvane, Sector 1, Nerul, Navi Mumbai 400 706
  E-mail: vivamumbai@vivagroupindia.net, Tel. 27721273, 27721274
- Jamals Fazal Chambers, 26 Greams Road, Chennai 600 006
  E-mail: vivachennai@vivagroupindia.net, Tel. 28290304, 28294241
- B-103, Jindal Towers, 21/1A/3 Darga Road, Kolkata 700 017
  E-mail: vivakolkata@vivagroupindia.net, Tel. 22836381, 22816713
- 7, Sovereign Park Apartments, 56-58, K. R. Road, Basavanagudi, Bengaluru 560 004
  E-mail: vivabangalore@vivagroupindia.net, Tel. 26607409, 26607410
- 101-102 Mughal Marc Apartments, 3-4-637 to 641, Narayanguda, Hyderabad 500 029
  E-mail: vivahyderabad@vivagroupindia.net, Tel. 27564481, 27564482
- Beevi Towers, First Floor, SRM Road, Kaloor, Kochi 682 018, Kerala
  E-mail: vivakochi@vivagroupindia.net, Tel: 0484-2403055, 2403056
- 232, GNB Road, Beside UCO Bank, Silpukhuri, Guwahati 781 003
  E-mail: vivaguwahati@vivagroupindia.net, Tel: 0361-2666386

www.vivagroupindia.com

Published by arrangement with
Thorogood Publishers Limited
10-12 Rivington Street
London EC2A 3DU,
UK

ISBN: 978-81-309-0508-2

Published by Vinod Vasishtha for Viva Books Private Limited, 4737/23, Ansari Road, Daryaganj, New Delhi-110 002.

Printed and bound by Raj Press, R-3, Inderpuri, New Delhi - 110 012.

The author

Martin Richardson is Director of Professional Development at Law South in the UK. He has a legal background, spending the first part of his career as a university lecturer and commercial contracts specialist. In the late 1980s, he moved to a major firm of City solicitors where he set up and ran the practice's education and training systems.

During the last ten years, Martin has undertaken a variety of management, consulting and training projects. He has led teams of varying shapes and sizes both national and international. His industry sector experience covers the professions, pharmaceuticals, manufacturing, the press and media, transport and NGOs.

In addition to his legal qualifications, Martin has an MBA degree and is a member of both the Chartered Institute of Personnel and Development and the Chartered Management Institute.

Contents

Introduction

It has occurred to me for some time that the bookshelf has been lacking a pragmatic, comprehensive yet challenging text to help people managers along that most difficult of paths – namely leading, motivating and running a team of people on a day to day basis.

People have personalities, people have intellects, people have emotions, people have demands, people are individuals – and to try and keep all these balls in the air, yet at the same time to move a group of people onwards as a unit – a team – requires the wisdom of Solomon coupled with the leadership skills of Aslan and the wizardry of Gandalf.

This book takes the form of a clinic during which a people manager asks an experienced people management consultant how he should approach particular issues and problems which form the bedrock of a manger's role and responsibilities. It can be read as a whole or dipped into as and when necessary. It could also act as a 'friend' and handy reference work.

I have tried to make it punchy in style and full of helpful tips and techniques, yet basing much of the advice on well regarded models. I hope therefore that it will be stimulating to peruse and will provide readers with pegs on which to hang their approach to managing their teams 'back at the ranch'.

Martin Richardson

ONE
Starting out

1.1 I have just been appointed to my first managerial post – and it's scary. How do I get over this apprehension?

To be apprehensive about such an important career move is quite natural. For the first time, you have been formally appointed to look after the working lives of other people – and 'people' is the key word here.

Up to now, you will probably have undertaken a particular technical role comprising the execution of tasks for which you had sole responsibility, and for the success of which you were accountable to your manager. Your focus was therefore on learning the skills which enabled you to develop excellence in doing those tasks free, generally speaking, from concern about your colleagues and how they were performing.

This task focus must now give way to **people focus**. The issue becomes of paramount importance if dealing with other people does not come naturally to you. Unfortunately, promotions to managerial roles are often made on the back of technical excellence rather than potential people skills.

In future your prime concern will be the members of your team and ensuring that the team as a whole performs effectively – and that means starting to learn new skills which help you to understand, motivate, develop, lead and communicate with a group of individuals with very different thoughts, feelings and outlook. If you should find people relationships difficult at this stage, you will need to put in serious effort to reinvent yourself as a manager and leader. The tips and techniques to help you do this form the substance of this book.

In summary, your former life will have probably focused 80% on the task and 20% on people; as a rule of thumb, your new role should begin to shift that ratio towards exactly the opposite position.

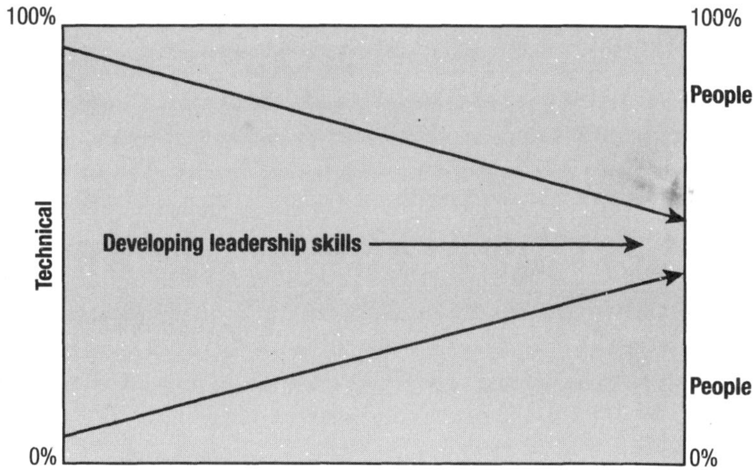

None of us likes the **process of change** very much and this is another cause for justified apprehension. However much you look forward rationally to your new role, adjustment to it and the new demands it makes upon you produces an emotional reaction.

The stages of transition follow a well recognized pattern. You start with a mixture of elation when told you've got the job and a 'what have I let myself in for' type of self-doubt. You then begin the role with an 'in fact, this is ok' type of false confidence approach (the honeymoon period), but quickly realize how much you need to learn and how demanding the role in fact is. At this point you may become quite anxious, realizing that the past has gone and that the future will require real effort to enable you to come to terms with the now permanent differences in your working life. It then requires serious effort to move out of this 'pit', but things will start to get better as you experiment with new ways of doing things, discover the management methods which best suit you and your team, and finally become totally integrated into your new role.

The transition process just described looks like this:

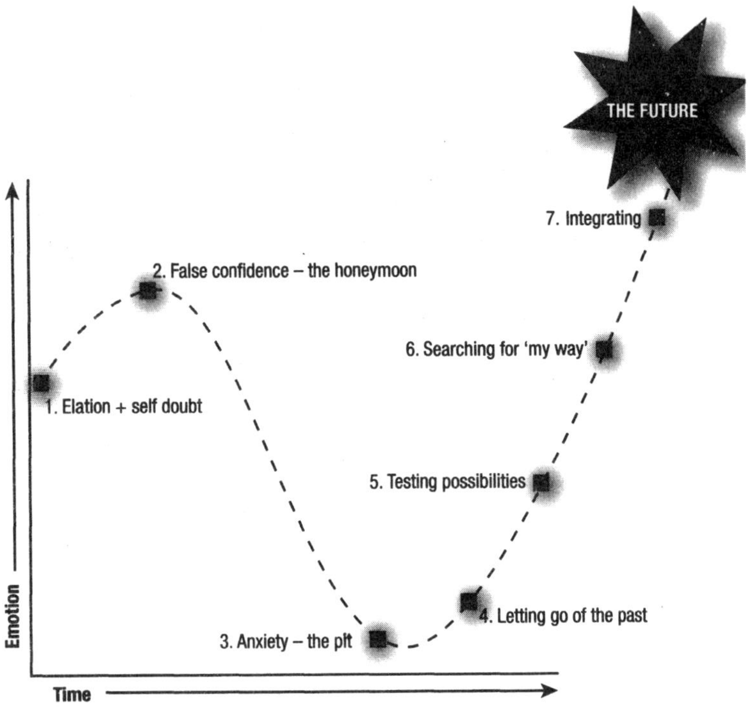

All those embarking on change should be aware of this process and that we are all subject to it.

1.2 What can I do ahead of starting the role to ease the transition?

Don't wait until Day 1 of the new job before thinking about what it will involve. Freshly appointed managers should do some basic background research before embarking on what will be a very different role.

The starting point should be the **job description**. You will have discussed what the job entails at your interview. Now get hold of the formal document and think through and visualize what each area of your responsibilities will look like. At this stage, you will gain an initial feel for both what is likely to go well fairly quickly and what may cause you a few problems as you get underway.

Next, find a **mentor**. This should be someone who has had experience in the past of undertaking the same sort of role. Your mentor could be within your organization or working outside it. In the case of the former, it should not be your line manager who would have conflicting interests in undertaking this dual role. Your mentor should be someone independent from your direct working life, someone with the wisdom and 'grey hairs' to advise you as to how you might proceed in problematic situations.

You will also find it useful at this stage to research the up to date **business plan** of your organization. This will give you the big picture of what your employer is all about and where the corporate future is perceived to lie. Learn the (currently unfashionable) mission statement; discover what the organization's values are; consider its goals, and the strategy it is using to implement the business plan.

Armed with this knowledge, you should now seek out your new **line manager** and discuss with him/her how your department's or function's activities lock into the big picture, what the priorities are and what is expected of you in the early days of your job. It will also be an opportunity to discover any particular problems you are likely to inherit and have to deal with at an early stage. Make sure you do not leave this meeting without taking with you any useful documentation which is likely to provide a more detailed insight into the issues you have discussed.

It would also be a good idea, ahead of starting if possible, or at the latest on the first morning if not, to meet **your team** as a group in an informal setting, just to be introduced/introduce yourself so that your team members can get a feel for the person they will be working with in future. Like speed dating, it is surprising how much one can sense and learn about a person within the first couple of minutes of meeting them. Don't underestimate the impact of that first team session.

It is less likely that you will meet individual **team members** ahead of starting, but you should certainly do this within the first week as part of your induction process. These meetings will enable you to find out about individual roles, and thoughts and feelings about how things are. They will also break the ice and significantly help with the 'people' issues and the development of your own thinking about your role and the future.

Case study

Michael was appointed to his first managerial role and took the steps outlined above to help him come to terms with his new responsibilities and to learn something about his team. One factor that came to light informally was that an older team member resented Michael's appointment and let it be known socially that he was going to give Michael a difficult 'testing out' when he started for real. Michael went to see the mentor he had selected and asked for advice as to how to handle this potentially damaging situation. His mentor made two or three suggestions, including giving the awkward team member some additional status and responsibilities. This took the negative wind out of the team member's sails, and what could have proved to be a difficult relationship got off to a more solid start than might otherwise have been the case.

1.3 I feel awkward about leading colleagues after being one of them for so long. How do I deal with this?

This question assumes that you have been promoted from within the team in which you currently work and now have responsibility for colleagues with whom previously you were 'one of the lads'.

This is indeed a tricky issue, and the solution involves a combination of developing respect and trust, and gradually creating some 'distance' between you and your team members.

It is highly probable that you will have been appointed in the first place partly because you already have the respect of your colleagues. If that respect was founded on your technical excellence, then you will need to be careful, since your new role is based on completely untried and untested managerial skills, hence the need to seek to develop these new skills as quickly as possible. Alternatively, you may have been viewed as a leader in waiting, in which case you may more naturally slip into the new role with the continuation and enhancement of pre-existing respect.

Trust will take time to develop. It will be based on your manifestation of competent managerial skills in an even-handed and fair manner within the team context, and, externally, of selling the team effectively to the outside world – internal and external customers. When team members come to see these skills consistently being displayed by you over time, their trust in you will grow and firm up. At the same time, they will relax into getting their jobs done without concern for the support they know they are receiving from you.

Trust and respect will inevitably and rightly produce some sense of **distance** between you and your team members. This is psychological distance born of the need to be able to exercise authority in those situations where you need to take a stance as leader. One ongoing example of this is your need to be able to give feedback on your team members' performance without fear or favour.

You will probably have socialized with team colleagues in the past. Continue to do so by all means, but when that Friday evening drinks session comes along, make sure you leave earlier than you would have done in the past before tongues become too loose and you may say something that adversely affects your credibility. Equally, seek out new networks outside the team. This will give you contacts with other managers with whom you will now have more in common from a daily work standpoint, and give you the natural opportunity to cut down your sessions with 'the lads'.

1.4 As a skilled technician, I don't want to abandon my technical skills entirely. What should I do?

Case study

Frank is a footballer in his mid-thirties. He has been and continues to be a great player for his club. He is held in high regard by his team mates. Following a typical, sudden departure of the manager, Frank agrees to take over. He begins his new role by continuing to include himself in the team for all the games, but soon realizes that the managerial responsibilities he has taken on are preventing him from fully concentrating on his footballing skills. Frank therefore concludes that if his playing days are to continue, he must drop back to a substitute's role. This he does, but again soon discovers that his fitness and on-the-field vision is deteriorating, and within six months of becoming team manager, he hangs up his boots and decides to concentrate his energies entirely on being a manager.

This is what is called the **player/manager syndrome**, and the footballing analogy applies equally to your own new role and how you are going to deal with it.

However, we live in a business age where the traditional concept of the people manager doing nothing but managing has gone. All managers are required to get their hands dirty to some extent, and this is why leadership, delegation and empowerment are now so important for the skilled manager to practice. Nevertheless, managing people effectively is a time consuming activity, and getting the balance right is critical. Depending on the size of your team and the nature of its work, you will be spending between no less than 40% and probably no more than 80% of your time on people management. Any less than 40%, and you will be failing in your role.

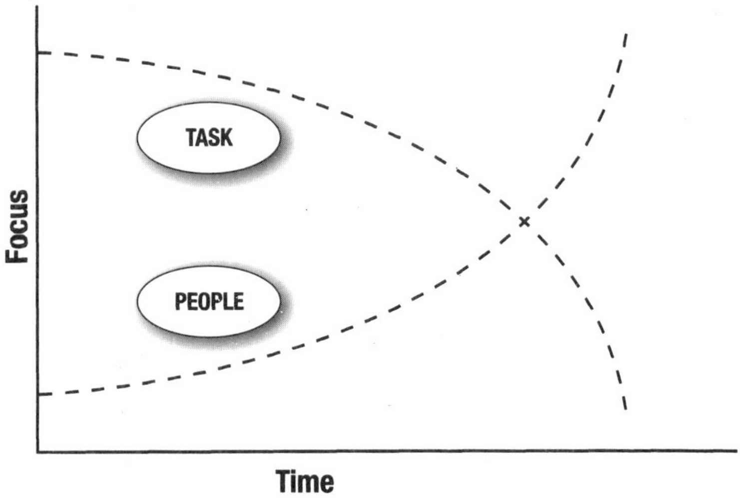

So the first word is of comfort to you – there will still be some technical tasks for you to do, but select their nature and amount wisely.

There are other ways to keep your hand in. Like Frank in the case study, one of your functions as a manager will be to coach your juniors. This in itself will keep your technical skills fresh. Equally, there may be occasions during holiday periods or temporary understaffing where you need to spend more time than usual back at the coal face. Or you could tackle technical issues from a completely different standpoint; for example, by setting up new operational systems and then monitoring and evaluating them.

Whatever you decide in terms of personal technical activity, remember that it is people management that is now your key function.

Summary

Here is a summary of some practical tips and techniques to help you over the scary period:

- Think through your task/people focus at present. Where am I on the scale and what must I do to help shift my focus?
- The change process will be difficult. Understand that to a greater or lesser extent you will follow the transition curve, and develop personal strategies to mitigate the effects of the 'down' periods.
- Read the new job description. This will put your planning into context and provide a framework.
- Find a mentor who has gone through this change before and seek their advice and wisdom.
- Begin by holding a general team meeting simply to say 'hello' so that the team can take an early view of how their new manager comes across. It is a truism that you can acquire a 'feel' for someone within the first minute of meeting them.
- Hold chats with all team members individually to find out about their roles, thoughts and feelings about how things are. These meetings will break the ice, and significantly help with the 'people' issues and developing your own thinking about your role and the future.
- Gain your team's respect and resulting trust by developing great managerial skills as soon as possible.

- Don't get too close to the team. Create some psychological distance to enable you to make people decisions without fear or favour.
- Break off your love affair with your technical skills and reduce it to one of simple friendship. Develop new and reduced ways of keeping your hand in with your technical expertise.

TWO
Team issues

2.1 I have inherited a team with which I have not worked before. How should I get to know the individual team members?

There are three things you should do which should help you learn more about your team members.

First, arrange **separate meetings** with each of them. This meeting will be similar in structure to a doctor's appointment – with you as the doctor. It will provide an opportunity to make a diagnosis of the team member – personality, strengths, weaknesses, likes, dislikes etc – by asking a variety of pertinent and incisive questions. In doing this, you will tease out a wealth of information on which you can base 'treatment'. This may range from 'everything is fine – carry on the good work' to some sort of change. In either case, do not rush to judgement or seek to make changes too soon. What you have heard may not always match observable behaviour and practice. Give everyone some time.

This leads to a further practical suggestion which is to try and find a task on which you can **work directly** with individual team members. This will provide you with a helpful insight into how the team member functions 'at the coal face' – technical ability, effectiveness, efficiency, communication skills, responsiveness, initiative etc. The information you glean can then be matched with that which you noted at the individual meeting. It puts you in a much stronger position to be able to argue the case for that team member's best fit within your team of the future.

Finally, think about a semi-formal **social event** for the team as a whole, for example, a drinks reception after work one evening. This type of occasion provides you with an opportunity to gauge how team members interact with one another as a group and how individuals behave when given an opportunity to 'let their hair down'. In the first case, you will discover whether the team is inherently content with its lot and also who seems to 'get on' with whom at a personal level. In the second instance, you may find differences in coping with a sense of personal responsibility. We all know how behaviour can change when the wine starts to flow. Any observations on this front may be added to the store of information upon which future decisions about management and leadership potential may be made. Remember, you must stay focused on a social occasion like this.

2.2 I wish to build and develop my team, and would like to use some analytical techniques to help me discover more about team members and to identify strengths, weaknesses and any skills gaps. How should I go about this?

This is potentially one of the most useful activities you can undertake when building and developing your team. It is impossible to have too much information on which to base team building decisions. The best tools to use for this purpose are **psychometric and other types of diagnostic testing**. The feedback you get from these exercises will be accurate validated assessments of team member capabilities. This information can then be added to the subjective views that you have gleaned from personal chats to provide a fully rounded profile of each team member.

The first question to ask yourself is: *what do you wish to test?* In general terms, there are three areas of interest to you: the technical skills required to do the job, the generic skills to support both the job and team activity, and behavioural issues which help to bind the team together as a cohesive unit of human beings. In all cases, you should be looking for strengths and how best to use them, balancing one team member's strength against another's weakness.

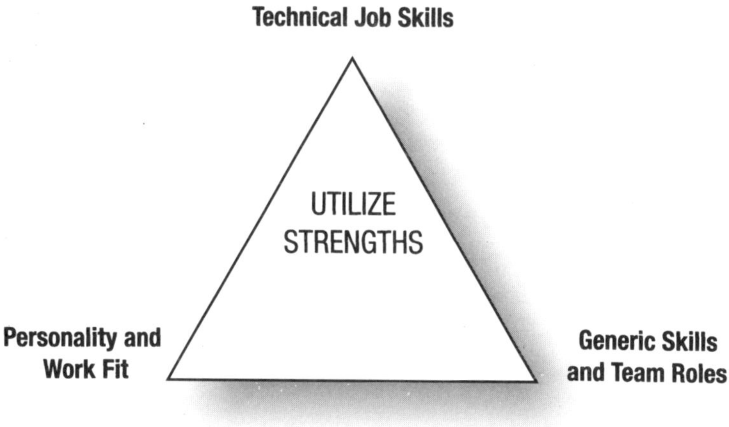

The Balanced Team

By doing this, you will maximize the value of what you do for your clients or customers and the business as a whole.

Technical skills. If recruiting (see 2.3 below), you will clearly wish to test technical skills ahead of appointment. If the technical skills include an understanding of a particular body of knowledge, you can check this by looking at the applicant's background and previous experience, and asking pertinent questions at interview. So a potential lawyer may be asked some basic questions about relevant legal principles and the latest changes in the law relating to a particular area of practice. You might also run an assessment centre with activities to test other technical skills such as (in the case of the lawyer) negotiating or public speaking. These skills are clearly core to the job and unless you are convinced that they already exist or can be readily addressed once the applicant is on board, you will not wish to recruit that particular individual.

For existing team members, technical competence can be tested 'on the job' and it will soon become clear who can and who can't. For those who can't, focused coaching and training should be introduced to bring these people up to speed. In the final analysis, the ability to perform at a technical level is paramount, and a strength somewhere along the required technical skills spectrum is essential.

Generic skills. These are those skills which are useful or even essential as an adjunct to technical skills. Their presence will enable the team member to do their job more efficiently and effectively and/or add value through a particular inherent skill to the functioning of the team as a whole.

Into the former category will fall, for example, **literary and numeric skills**. In both these instances, a variety of commercially available diagnostic tests exists which will help you to determine levels of competence in these areas. Literary skills are critical. Recent research has shown that, whatever the literary capabilities of the reader, corporate errors in spelling and punctuation in formal communications with customers are a serious blow to the potential for repeat business. In an era in which school focus has moved away from seeing literary accuracy as important, you may have some training and development work to do on this skill. Numeracy will be of importance to accounts, sales staff and others dealing with figures, but any problems here are mitigated by the simplicity of calculator use which effectively masks any basic lack of understanding.

The other area of generic skills concerns **effective team working**. According to Meredith Belbin, all of us have a variety of skills which assist with the general working practices and success of the team. Belbin has identified eight (he now adds a ninth – 'technical' – which seems to fit less well with the rest of the model) roles which, when put together as strengths, produce a fully rounded functioning team. The eight roles are:

- *Implementer* – the solid worker who can be relied upon to get things done
- *Co-ordinator* – often, but not always, the team leader who makes sure the team operates as a unit
- *Plant* – the sometimes eccentric very bright team member who produces creative ideas and keeps people intellectually on their toes
- *Monitor evaluator* – the analyst with an instinct for what will work and what will not
- *Completer finisher* – the perfectionist who dots all the 'i's and crosses all the 't's
- *Team worker* – the team's people person who keeps feathers from becoming too ruffled
- *Shaper* – the energetic entrepreneur type with a solid business instinct
- *Resource Investigator* – the team's networker and researcher who brings in information from the outside world

Individual team members often have strengths in more than one role, so provided all roles are covered, you can run a comprehensive Belbin team with less than eight members. Use the Belbin diagnostic to find out who is good at what roles in your team. What you are looking for as a result of undertaking this exercise is a skills balance. Get team members to complete the questionnaire themselves (self-perception), then cross check using a colleague for an objective viewpoint. Sometimes the skills we think we have are not necessarily the ones we are perceived to have. Also, people can develop particular Belbin role skills (and lose others) depending on the job they are currently doing and the skills demands that their job makes on them. As a career progresses, the tendency is for the

Belbin profile to flatten out and we are better able to undertake a variety of tasks using whatever role skills any particular situation demands.

The diagnostic and full details of the Belbin team role system are available on the Belbin website – www.belbin.com.

Behavioural and personality skills. This third element of team analysis concentrates on a team member's personality, his attitude to the way he works and his ability to fit in and relate to the general corporate culture, the specific working environment and relationships with other team members.

The best known and most widely used psychometric test used to determine personality traits is the *Myers Briggs Type Indicator (MBTI)*. It seeks to answer the question: 'Who am I?' This diagnostic seeks to place an individual in one of 16 personality types which are based on and adapted from the psychological work of Karl Jung. The 16 types are derived from the combination of four alternatives – **E**xtrovert v **I**ntrovert; **S**ensing v i**N**tuition; **T**hinking v **F**eeling; **P**erceiving v **J**udgmental. These alternatives represent, in the above order: how we absorb information, how we analyze that information, how we make decisions based on the analysis and how we implement those decisions in our daily lives. So each of us has a four letter description which identifies our type, eg INTJ. The accuracy of the results of the objective MBTI diagnostic is astounding, and the analysis of type extends not only to issues relating to behaviour at work but also many other standard aspects of our lives. In team terms, you can use these results to discover not only strengths and weaknesses, but also who gets on with whom and what types fit most suitably into your working environment. Full details are available from the Oxford Psychological Press website, www.opp.eu.com.

Another frequently used psychometric is *DISC analysis*. DISC uses a simple four box matrix which plots extroversion/introversion against a task/people orientation. So D stands for Dominance (extrovert/task); I stands for Influence (extrovert/people); S stands for Steadiness (introvert/people) and C stands for Compliance (introvert/task). DISC seeks to answer the question: 'How will I fit in?'

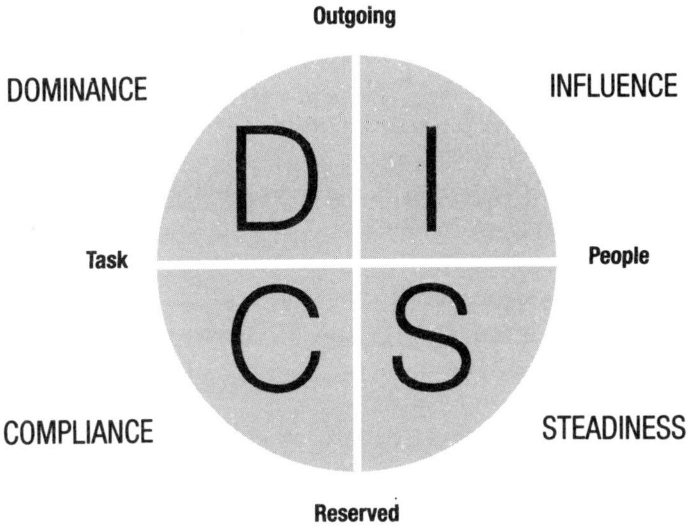

Personality at Work

The diagnostic analyses the team member's natural working preferences in graphical form. This can then be matched against the organization's own way of doing things by linking the individual's normal work mask to his reaction to stress. In recognizing that what follows is a sweeping generalization, the typical functional activities might place a high scoring D in an operations role, I as a marketeer, S an HR professional and C an IT specialist.

DISC analysis takes place solely online by completion of a brief questionnaire. It too produces some very useful results and can generate a variety of reports covering many human resource issues. Further details are available on the Thomas International website, www.thomasinternational.net.

Finally, you might wish to look at the *Margerison-McCann Team Management Wheel*. This model answers the question: 'What do I wish to do?' The wheel contains eight different types of work – promoting, developing, organizing, producing, inspecting, maintaining, advising and innovating. The work types are then locked into four types of personality – explorers, organizers, controllers and advisers. By doing this, the model seeks to match personality with work preference in order to ensure both diversity and balance within the team. As usual, you complete a diagnostic questionnaire to produce the results. Again, details are available from the 'tmsdi' website, www.tmsdi.co.uk.

The time spent learning as much as you can about your team members is time very well spent, allowing the people manager to set objectives and make decisions confident that they will work in human terms.

2.3 As part of my people management responsibilities, I sometimes need to recruit new members to replace staff who have left or to fill new gaps in the team. What is the process I should follow and how should I go about this recruitment exercise?

Whether to fill existing gaps, replace departing colleagues or as part of an expansion programme, recruiting the right new members into your team is a vital skill if only because errors are extremely costly.

Let's backtrack for a moment before considering how to proceed. Fortunately, most Western economies are now managed by a central bank which keeps a firm hand on the economic tiller through the judicious use and adjustment of *interest rates*. Interest rates are no longer a football kicked around by politicians. Consequently, the ups and downs of the economic cycle are much less pronounced than in the boom and bust eras of the past.

Under boom and bust, the tendency for organizations was to 'downsize' during bust and recruit madly during boom. The result was not only a *fluctuating workforce* that had no time to settle in properly and learn to perform really effectively for the long term benefit of the organization, but the costs incurred in redundancy payments (out) and recruitment agencies (in) were, and still can be, staggeringly high.

Although these significant employment up and downs seem at the moment to be a thing of the past, the first thing you should do as a people manager is *never to make any satisfactorily performing employee redundant except in totally unavoidable circumstances.* It is better to carry someone for a few months when times are tough and to have them trained, skilled and raring to go when the upturn comes, than go to the expense of redundancy and recruitment with all the attendant team management consequences that that entails.

So, assuming that you have a genuine and approved need to recruit, what process should you go through? Subject to liaising with and working alongside your HR department, here are the stages:

1. Write a **job description**. This is brief document, no more than one side of A4, which sets out in some but not total detail the nature of the role and the tasks and other activities that the job holder will be expected to undertake. It usually also includes where the role lies in the organization's line structure and thus to whom the person appointed will be reporting. This placing of the role will also help to fix a salary level. The job description is an important document. It helps you focus on what your real employment needs are, and it helps candidates determine whether the job is likely to be right for them.

2. Write a **person specification**. Again, one side of A4 will do. Here you will list the technical and personal skills together with any other competencies and experience which you are looking for in the ideal candidate. The person specification

will help you when sifting candidates and preparing for interviews.

3. **Advertise internally** for candidates. There may be suitable people currently elsewhere in the organization looking for a fresh challenge. There may even be someone in your own team who might be a potential choice. Encourage these people to apply. Not only will an internal appointment save you money, but the candidate will be already up to speed with the business culture and 'how we do things around here'.

4. **Look at cold call CVs**. Speculative resumes frequently fall on managers' desks. Make sure you keep and file those that look interesting, and at this stage, run through those you have kept to see if there are any possible matches. If there are, give these people a call to discover if they are still on the market.

5. **Contact recruitment agencies**. Failing a sufficient short list from within, talk to the recruitment agencies you normally use. Make sure that your chosen agency not only specializes in the type of role you are seeking to fill and the level of seniority it is pitched at, but also liaises with and understands your industry sector. If you reach this point, you are starting to spend money and you need to be sure that candidates put forward by the agency are sensibly entered at the starting gate, so make sure the agency works closely with the job description and person specification.

6. **Advertise externally**. Your recruitment agency will only advertise if they have no suitable candidates on their books. External advertising further pushes up costs, but may bring out of the woodwork some applicants who have not thought of moving but on impulse like the look of the role you are seeking to fill.

You could advertise externally, by-passing the recruitment agency stage. If you do, be prepared for a major administrative job in sorting the wheat from the chaff (of which there will be much) when the CVs start to roll in.

7. **Draw up a short list**. Alongside the recruitment agency, if you use one, pick a list of candidates who on paper look as though they could do the job effectively. A short list should comprise no more than six candidates and no less than three. These figures have a beneficial psychological impact for you as the recruiter, since the maximum number does not present so much choice that a decision becomes confusing and difficult, whilst the minimum number prevents a restrictive either/or situation which only two candidates would create. Also, be conscious of discrimination issues when short listing and comply with these and any other legal constraints, but do not indulge in positive discrimination. This is helpful neither for the organization not for the candidate. You must always seek to recruit the best candidate for the particular job.

8. **Decide assessment criteria**. There are a variety of recruitment tools which will help you reach a decision as to which may be the best candidate. No results are foolproof, but the use of two or more such tools will help to reduce the possibility of an erroneous decision. Pick any from:

   - Assessment centre
   - Psychometric testing
   - Skills testing
   - Group dynamics/interpersonal skills testing
   - Hands-on work experience
   - Interview

Which you choose will depend on a number of factors – the role itself, level of seniority, etc – but invariably there will be at least one formal face to face interview. If you intend to have a two stage recruitment process, do any testing in stage one plus an informal interview, possibly with you alone. Reserve stage 2 (for which you may have reduced a list of six to two or three) for meeting the team (will this candidate fit in?) and the formal interview which should comprise at least two interviewers. If your organization dictates the use of an interview panel, keep its numbers to an absolute minimum. Recruitment by a 'board' vote is bad practice.

9. **Make a job offer**. Assuming there ultimately is a candidate who is a good choice (and this is not always the case – readvertising is not uncommon, and never recruit someone simply for the sake of getting the job done), make them an offer of the job informally, ideally by telephone. If they are still interested in coming on board and are inclined to accept, get them into the office to discuss the detail – pay, holidays, other benefits etc – face to face and to answer any outstanding queries. When all this has been settled, write a formal offer letter containing the agreed terms and conditions, and keep your fingers crossed for a positive response. If after all this the candidate turns you down, there may be a runner up who in fact would be a good second choice. For this reason, do not turn down candidates who might be in this position until your number one choice has accepted. If you do, either you will be embarrassed or, worse, may well unnecessarily have to go thorough the whole costly process all over again.

2.4 I have a selection of CVs in front of me, all of which fulfill basic qualification criteria. How do I now go about whittling this pile down to a short list?

The first thing, as you say, is to ensure that the background and experience of the applicant is such that at first glance it marries up to the job description, i.e. he is able technically to take up the role. Having done that (and most applicants should match up in this way), here are some critical pointers regarding CV analysis which will help you end up with your six to go forward to the first stage:

- *Appearance*. Just look at the CV to start with. Is it pleasing to the eye? Is information set out in a logical manner? Is there plenty of white space? The layout of the document will tell you much about how organized an applicant is. Anything longer than two sides of A4 should be rejected.

- *Job focus*. Each CV that is written should be tailored to the particular application. Has the candidate set out his stall so that you can see it is your job he has focused on, or is it a standard form template which he is happy to send off whatever the job. Only put forward those who show that they have spent time thinking about your specific role.

- *Language*. Look for strong words like 'led', 'managed', 'organized' rather than bland or generic waffle such as 'liaised', 'involved in', 'helped with' when describing previous roles. You want people who can do things.

- *Historical timescales*. Check the work and educational experience. There should be no gaps between age 16 and the present. Months should appear alongside years, otherwise there is the potential for unaccounted periods of up to eleven months.

- *Inconsistencies*. Watch out for contradictory information, for example between information in the CV and a covering letter. Everything must match.
- *Correct ordering of material*. Most recent work experience should come first and the remainder set out backwards from there, becoming less detailed as the CV goes further into the past. Anything other than reverse chronology, or stressing experience way back in the past too heavily should be viewed with suspicion.
- *Over-statements*. Some applicants use words like 'best', 'top of', 'prize winner' in order to market themselves better. These words and phrases are meaningless unless backed up by statistical or comparative facts which put them into context.
- *Achievements*. You should be interested in positive outcomes arising from previous jobs and not simply a role description. Look out for hard words again like 'created', 'changed', 'adapted', which indicate proactive success.
- *Outside interests*. The presence of these in the CV ensures that you are not considering couch potatoes. Sometimes real achievement outside work is a positive indicator of future talent within work, particularly when a junior team member is being considered for a more senior role.

When you are satisfied that there are no serious problems arising in an application after checking it against this list of hazards, put it on the short list pile.

2.5 The interview is always considered the most important aspect of recruiting. How do I set up and run an effective recruitment interview?

The recruitment interview looks, on the face of it, to be a straightforward people management activity, but in reality is extraordinarily complex and time consuming.

The key issue underpinning all interview activity is to make it *as objective as possible*, so that the ultimate decision making is seen to be fair, judged from set criteria agreed beforehand and measured after the interview. Having said that, do not entirely ignore gut instinct. When all is said and done, you and your team must be able to work with the person appointed on a daily basis for what may be a long time.

The second initial point is that if you are intending to have two interviews – longer list followed by shorter list – make sure you *differentiate between the interviews*, perhaps by selecting particular issues to discuss at interview one, with more rigorous and searching matters left to interview two.

Here are some pointers which will help you ensure that your interviews are as thorough and effective as possible:

1. Plan rigorously

You cannot interview without detailed preparation. The matters you should be dealing with when planning an interview include:

- Select and invite the interviewing panel. The more senior the interviewers, the more credibility and importance is attached to the process and the job, so aim to have at least one senior person present.

- Select time, date and location. Do this well in advance to avoid clashes.

- Inform all parties – panel and applicant – when the event details are settled.

- Check with HR for any standard form documentation that your organization uses. If there is none, create your own. You should have as a minimum an interviewing checklist against which you can comment on and score factual information, including work based skills and personal qualities. Scoring is essential to ensure objectivity amongst panel members. Agree a scale, say 1 to 5, and define what each number represents – good, satisfactory etc.

- Create a list of relevant and pertinent questions. These should be phrased to test the skills and attributes which the job description and person specification list. For example:

  - *What's the most significant impact you've made in your current employment during the past twelve months? (testing achievement)*

  - *What ideas have you had which you have been able to implement during the past year? (testing initiative)*

  - *Describe a major difficulty you have faced this last year and how you overcame it. (testing perseverance)*

  - *Tell us about a failure in the last twelve months and the lessons you learnt from it. (testing character)*

- Distribute copies of all documentation, including CVs, to all interviewers at least two days in advance.

2. Before the interview

Make sure the interview room is set up correctly. A round table is ideal – you do not want to engender a 'you and us' atmosphere by having a candidate sitting opposite a row of strange people. The candidate is not here for a 'when did you last see your father?' grilling.

Interviewers should have a chat amongst themselves about how they see the interview being structured, who will test what skills and ask which questions, and generally to resolve any queries before the interview starts. Suppose you have six candidates. Ideally, one hour should be devoted to each, of which 45 minutes will be the interview itself and 15 minutes the pre and post interview chat between interviewers. This will provide you with enough time to complete the documentation and generally review how things are going.

3. The interview itself

The following steps will be helpful in ensuring that everything runs smoothly. Remember that this is a marketing exercise for your organization.

- Greet the candidate in reception yourself. Do not ask a secretary or other non-member of the panel to do it. It is intimidating for a candidate to enter an interview room 'cold' and this is not the reaction you want from him. Interviewing is not a power trip for the panel.
- Have a friendly 'pleasantries' conversation on the way to the interview room – how far have you come, did you find us ok, what was the traffic like etc. This will begin to relax the candidate and settle any nerves.
- Once in the room, seat the candidate and introduce the other members of the panel who should be encouraged to say a friendly 'hello'.
- Explain how the interview will be structured. Try this three phase approach:
  - Phase 1 – Examining past experience – 10 minutes
  - Phase 2 – Testing for role suitability – 30 minutes
  - Phase 3 – Candidate questions to the panel – 5 minutes
- Run the interview using this structure, having ensured beforehand that each panel member knows his role, when he will lead and what questions he will ask.
- Use your communication skills to maximum advantage. In particular, ask solid open and probing questions designed

to elicit as much information as possible that will enable you to judge effectively the candidate's suitability.

- Phase 3 is important. A good candidate will have two or three intelligent and incisive questions up his sleeve. Answer them honestly. Good questions asked could swing your decision in that candidate's favour.

- When all questions have been concluded, thank the candidate for coming and see him out with a comment that you will be in touch as soon as possible.

2.6 I have a new team to work with. In what ways can I expect the team to behave between the point that I take over and the time when I have helped to develop it into a fully effective operation?

All teams follow a life cycle. This lifecycle occurs not only when a team is put into place for the first time, but also when its membership changes, if only by one member. This is particularly true if that new member happens to be the manager.

The best known model to help understand this life cycle is Tuckman's view of group development. He identified four stages in the process – forming, storming, norming and performing. A fifth stage, mourning, could be added. This is a useful additional stage to think about when the team has been built for a specific project and disperses at its conclusion. The term 'reforming' might be more appropriate for a team that simply changes membership.

Watch out for these characteristics at each of the stages:

Forming

- A time of high uncertainty and hesitancy

- Still a group rather than a team

- Need to establish personal identities and make an impression
- Discussion as to who we are and why we exist

What you should do: communicate extensively with the group and its individual members and encourage open debate to settle anxieties and establish team thinking.

Storming

- Individual rivalries or even hostilities appear
- Personal agendas are revealed
- Overt challenges for doing things a particular way
- Need to agree specific objectives, roles and procedures

What you should do: use your powers of influencing and persuading to resolve personal issues and move the team towards agreement for future action.

Norming

- Individuality gives way to consensus
- Objectives clearly defined and decision making process resolved
- Behavioural and performance norms accepted
- Cooperation and trust begin to emerge

What you should do: move into a coaching mode to support progress, develop motivation and iron out any remaining problems.

Performing

- Harmonious working relationships
- High performance and motivation
- Focus on achievement

- Mature approach to task and communication

What you should do: become the genuine leader, delegating and empowering as much as possible.

Mourning/reforming

- Project winds up/team member leaves
- More extremes of emotion – elation/loss
- Uncertainty of change
- Break up of working relationships

What you should do: sensitively manage the change, stressing fresh future challenges – new projects/integration of new team member.

The time scale for going through the full cycle will vary. In the case of a time constrained project, you should manage the team through stages one to three as quickly as possible, arriving at four in the shortest possible time frame. Where the team is permanent, it is possible to spend a little more time ensuring that things are right, although change here will normally be the exit and arrival of one team member. You should seek to integrate this single fresh face as quickly as possible. If fresh faces keep appearing with some regularity, you must ask yourself 'what's wrong with my team and what must I do to put things right?'

2.7 I've built my team and it is up and running. What signs and symptoms should I look out for which will tell me that all is going well (or not, as the case may be)?

The effective team manifests a number of clear characteristics which you should be seeking to develop and maintain. Equally, you need to be sensitive to any deviation from these characteristics and be prepared to rectify problems before they become real issues. By committing to these principles, you will have ensured that members have moved on from being simply a group of discrete individuals to a well-rounded team.

Here are the **Top 10 Characteristics of Successful Teams** which you should be developing and monitoring. As you go through the list, make a note of any which may not be all they should be at the moment:

- A shared commitment to clear goals and objectives
- All team members participate fully in achieving those objectives
- Your leadership is flexible in style, and you manifest an approachable personality
- All team members buy into decision making
- Communication amongst team members is open and honest; in particular, everyone is a good listener
- All team members feel empowered to contribute ideas and thoughts and to work to their best of their ability
- Everyone is supportive and trusting of each other – there is an emotional input to good team relationships
- There exists in the team enthusiasm and a willingness to take calculated risks
- Problems and issues are resolved rapidly (some disagreements are a fact of life)
- The team is able to evaluate its own effectiveness and adapt to change

On the other hand, a failing team will be operating in exactly the opposite way to the above. You might also look out for the following additional potential negative behaviours: Individual aggression; competition for 'airtime'; concentration on ego rather than task achievement; political machinations; failure to have regard for timelines.

Should any of these negatives exist, you should take immediate remedial action to solve the problem.

It will by now have become very clear that, as a people manager, you have a highly responsible, challenging and time consuming role. Developing the skills to do the job effectively is thus vitally important.

Summary

Here is a summary of some practical tips and techniques to help you deal with team issues:

- Get to know your team members as soon as possible. Meet them individually, organize a social event and work directly with some of them.
- Do some analysis to identify strengths and weaknesses in the team. Assess technical, behavioural and generic team skills using psychometric and other forms of testing.
- When you need to recruit, make sure you follow a procedure which will ensure you end up with the best candidates. Produce a job description and person specification. Advertise appropriately, draw up a shortlist and determine your assessment criteria.
- Institute a sifting process for CVs which will ensure the best possible short list. Consider issues such as job focus, work history, positive language and a rounded life – not forgetting the overall appearance of the document.
- Structure the interviews effectively so that you ultimately choose the best. Plan carefully and, on the day, put the candidate at ease and ask incisive open questions to elicit the maximum of helpful information.
- Once the team is in place, move it forward to become an efficient and smooth running operation as soon as possible. Be aware of the forming, storming, norming and performing phases, managing each one with a view to the next step in mind.

- Be aware of and develop the Top 10 Characteristics of Successful Teams that will indicate to you that your team is productive, happy and well motivated.

THREE
Leadership

3.1 As a manager, I am expected to supervise and lead. What is the difference between managing, leading and supervising?

This is a good question. The boundaries between these three activities are blurred, thus to define each with clarity presents difficulties. Indeed, some people have used and continue to use the terms 'management' and 'leadership' interchangeably. However, it is possible to draw some important distinctions which will help you to define your role more precisely.

Management should be seen as a generic term. It is a broad based function which can describe any activity taking place within the business. Thus, I manage my time, I manage my team, I manage my project, I manage operations. The underlying message from the use of this term is one of administration. It has a reactive ring to it which smacks of implementing decisions made elsewhere. It does not conjure up a picture of dynamism, initiative or creativity. It is much more concerned with coordination, structuring and processing. A manager in this sense is, typically, desk bound and surrounded by paper and people asking questions. On its own, this type of management is now an outdated form of working. The last great raft of such managers in the UK lost their jobs in the recession-driven clear out of the early 1990s.

Leadership, on the other hand, is proactive. This word conjures up energy and forward thinking. It implies followership, thus a leader is recognized as such and respected by the members of the team. It is therefore a direct people function, unlike management which is more abstract and conceptual. A leader has vision, is able to motivate those with whom he comes into contact and inspires trust and confidence. In particular, a good leader creates the right team for the job in hand and then empowers its members by communicating and delegating effectively, leaving himself free to drive forward the big picture. Examples of great leaders include Churchill (WWII), Ghandi (Indian politics), Brearley (English cricket, 1981), Thatcher (Conservative politics), Mandela (South African politics) and Branson (business). Notice that there is no common type of personality in this brief list. But all have their own brand of charisma which creates followership and ultimate success for the vision.

Leadership, therefore, is a central and critical element in successfully managing businesses and the people who work in them; management, on the other hand, encompasses a much broader and less dynamic spectrum of responsibility and activity.

Where then does **supervision** fit in? This term is usually reserved for first line functional responsibilities where the supervisor supervises the quality output of front line operatives. So, using traditional language, a foreman of a gang of refuse collectors has what is essentially a supervisory role. He runs the way in which that gang collects refuse. In this sort of scenario, it is unlikely that a supervisor will have direct people management responsibilities. Normally supervisors themselves report to a first level people manager. But what supervisors do do is to advise and coach those for whose operational success they are responsible, and thus have a crucial technical development role to play.

Case Study

Archie is a partner in a firm of lawyers. He is Head of the Real Estate Department. Apart from doing a small amount of top level fee-earning work himself, his main role is to lead, manage and supervise his team members. Archie **leads** them by thinking ahead strategically and discussing and deciding on future courses of action with his team members – potential growth areas, new target clients, increased turnover, any changes in practice focus, i.e. he produces a business plan for the team. Archie also **manages** his team members by organizing day to day operational issues – who does what, sorting out budgeting and resourcing matters, monitoring performance, dealing with personal issues and generally keeping day to day matters on track. Finally, Archie spends some time at the desks of his junior fee-earners and trainees, passing on his experience and words of wisdom as they get to grips with developing their technical expertise; .i.e. he **supervises** their work. As part of his leadership responsibilities, Archie may well delegate to and empower some of his more senior assistants much of this coaching role.

3.2 So now I am a manager, what exactly should I be doing in general terms of a day to day basis?

One of the best models to help in answering this question is John Adair's 'action- centred leadership'. The very title of the model sets the tone – that in carrying out your responsibilities, you should be manifesting the key traits of the talented leader, namely pragmatism and energy.

So what are those responsibilities? According to Adair, there are three elements to your role on which you should be concentrating:

- the *task(s)* that your team exists to accomplish
- the *team* which is put together to achieve your goals
- the *individuals* whose development as members of the team is crucial to the ongoing success of team activity

Each of these three points of focus are in fact interrelated and do not stand alone. Adair illustrates this graphically by presenting his model as three interlocking circles.

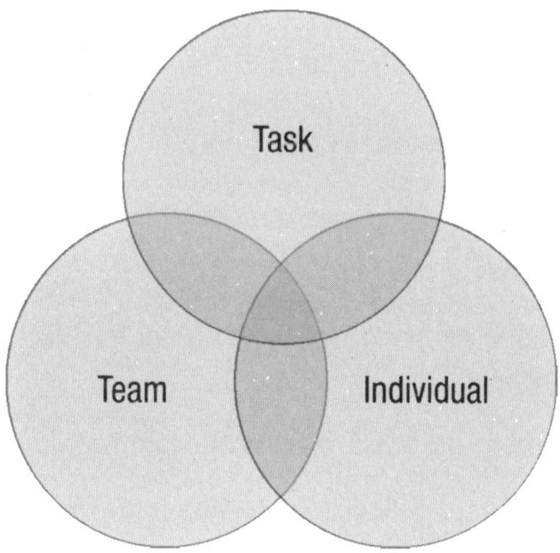

Action-centred Leadership

So what in particular is involved here? Here are a few practical matters which you should address within each circle:

Achieving the task

- Make sure what you are seeking to achieve fits in with organizational objectives
- Define the task and communicate it to all stakeholders clearly
- Create a plan of action using team roles and the particular strengths of team members
- Ensure all resources are in place – budgets, timescales, physical items etc
- Check lines of authority and remove any possible organizational barriers
- Set targets, deadlines and milestones then monitor progress
- Evaluate the finished product and file lessons learnt for future reference

Managing the team

Consult, involve, communicate, explain (CICE) in as many of these activities as possible:

- Setting team objectives
- Deciding how to achieve objectives
- Motivating the team
- Holding regular (brief) meetings for feedback and monitoring purposes
- Keeping the team abreast of organizational issues
- Making team decisions on day to day matters
- Celebrating success

Developing individuals

- Set targets at performance review meetings
- Provide relevant training and coaching
- Utilize and broaden job skills
- Create challenges through job enrichment activities
- Motivate by showing interest and praising efforts
- Be approachable
- Recognize publicly individual achievements

These lists are clearly not comprehensive, but will give you a grounding in some of the areas in which Adair sees an action-centred leader undertaking the role. Further, you will notice that there is some clear overlap between activities within the three elements of the role; e.g. motivating, objective setting and planning, and this is reflected in the interrelationship of the circles in the model.

3.3 I am part of what we call a matrix organization. Will the leadership skills that I need to develop in this environment differ from those I would use in a traditional organization?

A so-called matrix organization is one where traditional corporate departmental activities cross-integrate on a daily basis with on-going project activities. The result is that team members who have line management accountability to the departmental head, in fact often work on a temporary daily basis within a particular project team. This is how the matrix might look:

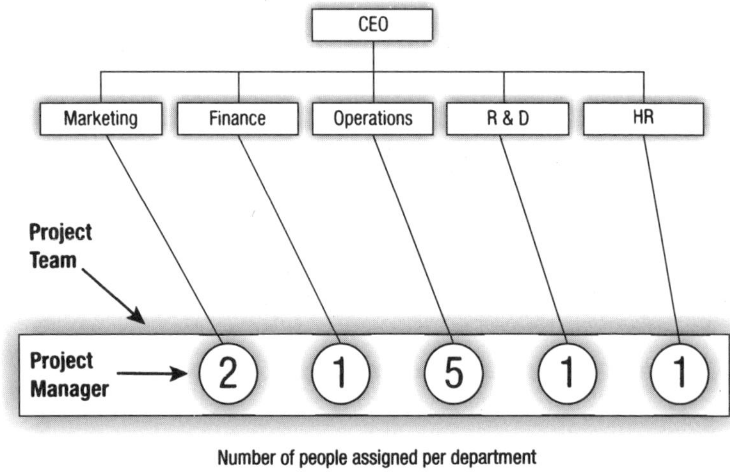

The Project People Resource – Matrix Organization

Matrix organizations are often found where skills need to be taken from a pool and concentrated into a single project.

Examples

1. A large firm of accountants acting as part of a major corporate finance deal will require not simply banking, capital transfer, tax and audit input, but also employment, property and pensions expertise taken from elsewhere on a temporary basis.

2. A builder, often acting as a sole trader, will pull in demolition, brick-laying, plastering, electrical and plumbing expertise as he needs it from other usually sole traders, during the course of a construction project.

Notice from these examples that sometimes the matrix team is made up of members from outside the organization who are not on the payroll as well as internal employees.

As a **line manager** running a centralized department, you will act as a traditional people manager, leading the permanent team you have put together and with continuing responsibility for recruiting, training, promoting and career development. Your team members wherever they are working still report directly to you. It follows that your team as a major project resource provides you with significant organizational power, and you must use that power wisely. Do not be too precious about team members, but develop an outgoing relationship with project managers, asking 'how can I help?' rather than clinging jealously or unhelpfully to your people.

As a **project manager**, on the other hand, you have no direct control over your temporary team members. You must therefore develop as a critical skill the ability to influence and persuade in order to get things done and make things happen. In delegating specific project tasks, you must recognize and respect the expertise of your team members, their line status and team of origin. Top class communication skills are essential to manage potential issues of conflicting loyalties and de-motivation. Remember that some of those allocated to you may not really wish to be part of your project. This influencing approach is essential because in the final analysis, you cannot pull rank as the ultimate sanction.

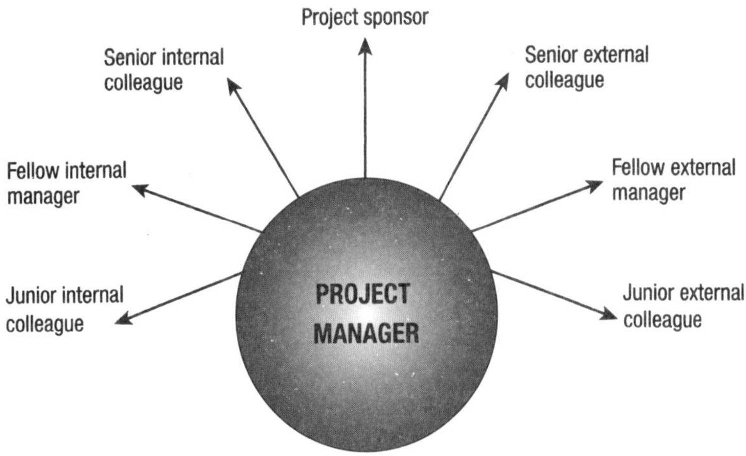

The Peacock Fantail of Matrix Management Relationships

3.4 I work in an organization which has multiple offices spread over a wide area. Some of my team members are located in these remote offices. What particular practices should I adopt to ensure that I manage my team effectively even though they are working at a distance from me?

The situation you describe is now common. Whether your remote team is confined within national boundaries or is global, there are key issues you need to consider which arise solely because you do not have the opportunity to have face to face interaction with all your people on a daily basis.

The overarching requirement when managing remote teams is to **build trust**. Trust is critical in terms of empowerment, delegation and generally getting the job done. These leadership skills become even more important when it is impossible to keep an eye on everyone all the time, and the creation of ongoing trust is built on **respect** for your ability to manifest solid leadership traits.

So what does this mean in practical terms?

1. **Understand the make-up of your team.** Remote teams comprise a variety of individuals with patent differences. Quite apart from the standard issues of gender, race and religion endemic in all teams, additional cultural factors arise in the remote situation.

   Even *nationally* this is the case. In the UK, a people manager of a remote team based in London with direct reports located in Newcastle and Liverpool must be sensitive to geordie and scouse cultural approaches to getting the job done. The same applies in the US where team members are located in, say, Boston, Houston and Minneapolis.

   Where the team is *global*, these problems are magnified. A team comprising US, Japanese, Greek, Indian, German, Swedish and Spanish people requires particular leadership sensitivity.

2. **Learn and work with key cultural differences.** In the global context, Hofstede identified five particular opposing factors which you should be aware of and manage appropriately:

   - *Power v. distance,* i.e. manage via tight hierarchical control (power) or via distributed empowerment (distance). Malaysia, Russia and Mexico are examples of the former; UK, Denmark and New Zealand of the latter.

   - *Structure v. uncertainty,* i.e. manage via strict procedural rules (structure) or via ambiguity and acceptance of risk (uncertainty). Greece, Guatemala and Poland fall into the first category; Ireland, Sweden and Singapore into the latter.

   - *Individualism v. collectivism,* i.e. manage the specific task, skills and employee (individualism) or the whole team as a social network (collectivism). US, Australia and Hungary are individualistic; Taiwan, Pakistan and Venezuela are collectivist.

   - *Masculine v. feminine,* i.e. manage competitively and with a results orientation (masculine) or caringly with concern for people issues (feminine). Japan, Switzerland and Jamaica are masculine examples; Thailand, Costa Rica and Sweden, feminine.

   - *Long term v. short term,* i.e. manage for future business relationships (long term) or for immediate commercial gain (short term). Oriental countries are examples of the former; western nations of the latter.

   Keep these differences very much in mind when working with your international colleagues, and note that there are many different combinations of approach depending on the particular country with which you are dealing.

3. **Communicate appropriately.** Research has shown that those organizations which work remotely, yet have the most proactive internal communications strategy, are the happiest and most successful. In particular, it is important for such businesses to use all the communication methodologies available to them to best advantage. These are some specific communication matters for you to consider:

    - *Face to face conversations.* Immediately, you have here the key problem. It is impossible for you to see people whenever you wish. The more dispersed the team, the more costly in both real and time terms it is for you to travel to see team members. Nevertheless, you must meet your team sometimes and your organization must recognize that the costs involved are essential if the team is to function effectively. Think about this list as the occasions on which you must see people:

        - When first appointed to your people manager role. In this instance, you should visit each outlying location so that you get to understand not only the team members themselves but also the environments in which they work.

        - Appraisals. These critical people management meetings can only be held face to face.

        - Team meetings not less than every six months. These can be held in the most convenient location (e.g. hotel at an air hub) to which everyone can most easily fly.

        - To sort out specific work issues where face to face contact is clearly most appropriate.

      On this basis, you should see all direct reports in the flesh roughly once every three months. This applies to international teams; if your team is dispersed solely within national boundaries, aim for once a month.

- *Video conferencing*. If available, use this as a back up, *but not as a replacement*, to face to face contact. Use it, perhaps, for some of the work issue conversations and as an occasional alternative to the telephone. But remember there are technical limitations to video conferencing as a communication tool, and also some people simply cannot cope in front of a camera.
- *Telephone/tele-conferencing*. This is the next best medium after face to face. Make sure you speak to all direct reports at least once a week. Be particularly sensitive to spoken accents when on the telephone. Listen carefully and try to attune your ear to how your overseas team member expresses himself. There are a multitude of accents and nuances in which English, as the main international language, can be spoken.
- *Email*. The key thing here is not to overuse it. When it is appropriate, again be aware of linguistic and spelling difficulties which team members from other cultures may have. There will also be differing forms of expression. A US email may be brief and to the point; an oriental email may be prolonged for the sake of courtesy.
- *Intranet and specialist team sites*. Use these to maximum advantage. Develop your IT systems as a comprehensive communication medium. Include team membership information with photographs, organizational news, team project news, team member news (gossip columns not only satisfy human nosiness but also tell us interesting titbits about our colleagues) and a help line which may include a blog or chat line. And keep it up to date!

4. **Develop those specific remote leadership skills.** Here are some of the major abilities, attitudes and traits you should be using as a remote manager:
    - *Abilities:* to listen effectively, to hold meaningful conversations, to develop excellent language skills, to cope with misunderstandings, to initiate interactive conversations and to use well honed interpersonal skills.
    - *Attitudes:* to develop cultural empathy, to respect local cultures, to be sensitive to local politics, to be non-judgmental and to be understanding of different ways of doing things.
    - *Traits:* seek to develop patience, tact, perseverance, tolerance and maturity.

By taking these actions and skills into account, you will find that managing your remote team becomes not only successful but enjoyable.

3.5 What behavioural style should I adopt when leading my team?

As human beings, we all have different personalities developed from unique genetic, environmental and social experiences, and this personality reflects itself in a particular manner when we are handling our relationships with other people.

As it gets to know you, the team will learn to respond in a certain way as a result of the style you adopt. They will know what to expect when you deal with them in standard day to day business situations, and this style will reflect your personality and thus your preferred way of relating to other people.

Unfortunately, sticking with this single approach will not always work, since the leadership demands which you are now facing present a variety of challenges requiring different ways of managing both your team as a whole and its individual members. You must therefore be able to adjust your style depending on particular business circumstances.

The classic model which best describes and helps you adapt to differing management demands is the **Situational Approach** model. What is does quite simply is to plot the amount of support you should be giving the team or an individual member of the team against the amount of formal direction the team or that person needs in the particular situation regarding the activity presently being carried out. The resulting four box matrix gives you four differing styles of leadership to use – ordering, coaching, delegating and empowering, as below.

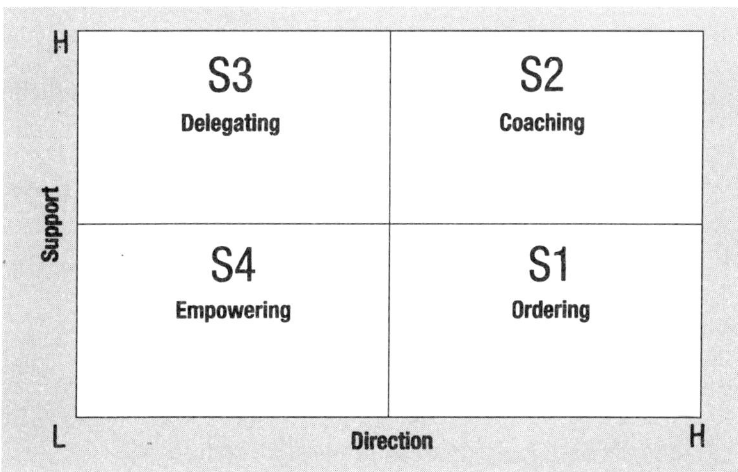

Leadership Styles

Two points immediately follow from this. Firstly, it becomes clear that you cannot use your preferred style in all management situations, and secondly, you should adopt and move around the four styles flexibly as circumstances demand.

So when might you use each of the four styles? Here are few ideas on each.

Ordering S1 (low support; high direction). In this situation, speedy action is necessary. It is the classic style to adopt when 'fire-fighting' or when attempting to meet a very tight deadline where there is no room for individual manoeuvre. As leader here, you will simply tell people what to do and then let them get on with it. You might also use the ordering style to push home a message to a particular team member who is unnecessarily and temporarily underperforming for no clear reason. Again, it may be appropriate when bringing a new team member up to speed with 'the way we currently do things around here'. Use this style as sparingly as possible; ordering people about is not now considered good management practice. But the ordering style will be accepted by team members in those limited situations where it is essential to achieve a necessary outcome.

Beware: misuse of the ordering style turns you into a dictator

Coaching S2 (high support; high direction). As this style indicates, its classic use is for coaching purposes. You will need to employ this style when skills training at the workstation or implementing new processes and procedures into the team. It will also be useful in other areas of personal development, for example, talking through career development opportunities, job enrichment activities or sorting out a team member's work/life balance problem. In all these last situations, you will not only be supporting your team member but also advising them as to possible solutions.

Beware: misuse of the coaching style turns you into a nanny or fusspot

Delegating S3 (high support; low direction). This is in many respects the ideal style to be in when circumstances allow. As a leader, you will have developed your team objectives and implementation plan, have identified team member strengths and skills and have allocated tasks accordingly. With everything running smoothly, you have effectively delegated those tasks to team members who know what they are doing. You therefore let them get on with the job, subject only to a standard monitoring and review structure which as a skilled delegator you will have naturally put into place when briefing them. Thus the team member is enabled to get on with the work without direction, but yet has you as a supportive manager available to deal with any unsolvable problems and to keep an eye on how things are going. The success of this style, therefore, is dependent on your skills as an effective delegator.

Beware: misuse of the delegating style turns you into a lifeguard, only taking an interest when things go wrong.

Empowering S4 (low support; low direction). In some senses, this is a scary style to adopt. To empower effectively, your team member must not only be both technically totally competent, and also the sort of person who is generally capable of looking after themselves in getting all aspects of their job done well whilst keeping you up to date with progress. It is a style that can more readily be adopted with senior positions and roles. It can also be used where you take over a team containing very experienced members who have the skills and, possibly, the psychological need to continue to plough their own helpful furrow – at least for the time being. In short, the key need is for the manager to be able to trust totally the team member's hands-on ability and sense of responsibility. Ideally, the empowerment style should be one that a manager aims to achieve with all team members in due course, after developing them through styles one to three first.

Beware: misuse of the empowerment style turns you into an abdicator of responsibility.

3.6 As a team leader, I know that one of my main functions is to motivate my team. What are the key issues that I should concentrate on in order to keep my team happily moving our objectives forward?

Motivation is what makes a team member want to do something. It is a vital state of mind if your team is to produce top quality results. Without motivation, team members will not give of their best, even when all the resources they need are in place.

It is your responsibility as team leader to ensure that your people are well motivated, either by directly creating the right psychological environment in which your people can flourish, or by empowering them to motivate themselves through developing a sense of personal responsibility for their own achievements. The more senior the team members, the more likely it is that you can put into place the second of these alternatives.

This difference between the 'hands on' and 'hands off' approach to motivation can be illustrated by looking at **McGregor's** so called **X – Y theory**. This states that all people can be divided into two camps: those who have to be told what to do (X) and those who respond to being empowered to get on with their job (Y). To motivate these two groups, people managers must actively direct the former but simply positively influence the latter – a 'carrot and stick' approach to motivation.

Here are some of the differences between the two types of managerial thinking:

TYPE X	TYPE Y
People are naturally lazy; they will avoid work if they can.	People are naturally active; they enjoy striving to meet agreed objectives.
People expect and depend on direction from above; they do not want to think for themselves.	People close to the action see and feel what is needed and are capable of self direction.
People should concentrate on their specific jobs; larger policy issues are none of their business.	People demand ever increasing understanding; they need to grasp the big picture surrounding their activities.
Most people have little intellectual ability and are generally unimaginative.	The intellectual and creative ability of most people is underused.
The driving force behind working is the fear of being demoted or fired.	The main reason why people are productive is a desire to achieve their personal goals.

McGregor's views are becoming rapidly antiquated when set against first world working conditions of the 21st century. The need for a type X approach, particularly when applied to people doing mindless, boring and repetitive jobs on a production line, is rapidly disappearing as robotics increasingly take over these tasks. The need for intelligent working at all levels within a society which now balks at being told what to do demands a type Y approach in most situations. There will, of course, be occasions when one of your team members may need a reminder of 'what it's all about', but by and large, empowering through influencing is now the order of the day. This underpins the fact that people management is a seriously skilled role to carry out successfully. Influencing and communicating to achieve team goals is a far more difficult proposition than simply treating team members like robots and telling them what to do. In fact, McGregor's X – Y theory now tells you more about your own instinctive attitude to people management than it does about your team members' approach to their work. Beware the X in you.

Much more helpful to you in a broad context is **Maslow's Hierarchy of Needs**. This motivational approach applies to life in general and is based on an instinct which tells us that we must satisfy certain basic needs in our lives before moving on to satisfy higher level needs. This 'ladder' of needs is usually set out as a pyramid like this:

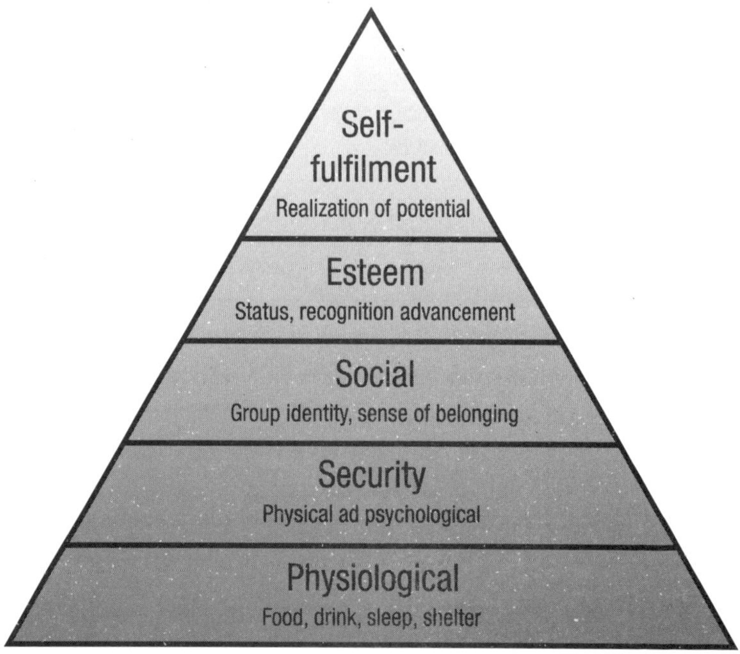

Maslow's Hierarchy of Needs

So our physiological needs must be in place before we can move on to satisfy psychological needs and so on up to level five at the top of the ladder. Thus, each level provides a foundation for the next level above. Fortunately, most of us have the first two levels solidly in place for most of our lives, but we do tend to move up and down quite frequently within the top three levels. In the work context, consider these issues where Maslow may be of help:

Examples

1. One of your team members is appearing somewhat remote and is underperforming. There may be a psychological problem here. Does he really enjoy his job or has he discovered that he is a square peg in a round hole, or is he worrying about a lack of coaching? More importantly, does he have a problem outside work – a difficult relationship or family bereavement for example – which could be adversely affecting performance? If so, these psychological problems must be sorted out before the team member can return to focusing properly on his job at the next level.
2. A new team member is spending much of his time looking lost and lonely. Are you spending enough time ensuring that he is properly welcomed and given the right opportunities to fit into the team? In other words, are you correctly addressing what may be a level three social need? This needs to be sorted out before he can think about moving up to the next performing level.
3. One of your harder working team members never looks happy but never complains. Is there a level four esteem problem here? Are you publicly providing the recognition that your team member needs to show that he is much appreciated and does a good job? Only when this happens can the team member start to feel fulfilled.
4. Your experienced high flyer has begun to look listless and bored. He has reached the self fulfilment stage at level five. Have you got a new and stimulating challenge that will take him back to level four so that he can take a fresh aim at level five? Or is the reality that it is time for him to move on to pastures new (that would mean his going back to level three in a different organization)?

Probably the most helpful motivational model for use at work is that developed by **Herzberg**. Herzberg took a series of factors which were generally accepted as work based motivators and analyzed them into two discrete lists.

The first list, he suggested, were not true motivators, but rather what he called 'hygiene factors'. The effect of these was to entice you into the organization and, so long as they remained in place, they would keep you there but no more. Once a key hygiene factor was removed for whatever reason, you would immediately start to look around for a new role.

The second list, Herzberg thought were the true motivators – the factors which team leaders and team members should strive hard to ensure were in place, for it is these that give you a buzz in the morning and a keenness to get into work and get the job done on an ongoing basis.

Here are Herzberg's lists:

HYGIENE FACTORS	TRUE MOTIVATORS
Corporate culture	Achievement
Good management	Recognition
Fair pay and benefits	Interesting and meaningful work
Pleasant colleagues	A sense of responsibility
Good working environment	Personal development

The effect of all this on you as a people manager is to make sure that you focus on the list on the right. Thus:

- agree sensible objectives and targets at formal reviews so that team members can feel that sense of achievement over time;
- make sure that when a piece of work or project is done well, there is praise, thanks (and reward where appropriate) and that this is in the public domain so that the team member feels pride and recognition for what had been completed;

- as far as possible, ensure that each team member's job is as stimulating as possible. Try job rotation if things can become a little tedious. Interesting and meaningful work is a tried and tested turn on;
- as a leader, use your ability to empower team members so that they can enjoy the responsibility of their role. With your support, that responsibility will seem not only perfectly tolerable but will instil a sense of worth. Eventually, your team member will be able to take on yet more responsibility as part of their own management development;
- ensure that you and your team member look to the future and agree a career development programme for him within the business. Failure to do so will result in the loss of that employee. Individuals should own their own career plans, but a little help from you could keep your team member focused on your organization in this context, and not necessarily looking to move on.

Self-test

If you are uncertain as to which of the Herzberg motivators turns you or your team member on most, try this forced pair comparison (see question 3.7) below. For each pair, tick the one which you think is the greater motivator for you, then when you have finished, count the ticks for each motivator to give you a preferred result. This produces a much more objective result than trying to pick one 'blind' from a list of eight possibilities.

Personal Development	OR	Good Working Conditions
Achievement	OR	Responsibility
Like-minded Colleagues	OR	Achievement
Responsibility	OR	Stimulating Work
Achievement	OR	Personal Development
Good Working Conditions	OR	Fair Pay
Responsibility	OR	Like-minded Colleagues

Fair Pay	OR	Responsibility
Recognition	OR	Personal Development
Achievement	OR	Fair Pay
Stimulating Work	OR	Achievement
Good Working Conditions	OR	Responsibility
Like-minded Colleagues	OR	Fair Pay
Stimulating Work	OR	Like-minded Colleagues
Personal Development	OR	Responsibility
Fair Pay	OR	Recognition
Like-minded Colleagues	OR	Personal Development
Achievement	OR	Good Working Conditions
Recognition	OR	Like-minded Colleagues
Fair Pay	OR	Stimulating Work
Like-minded Colleagues	OR	Good Working Conditions
Recognition	OR	Achievement
Responsibility	OR	Recognition
Personal Development	OR	Fair Pay
Stimulating Work	OR	Good Working Conditions
Recognition	OR	Stimulating Work
Stimulating Work	OR	Personal Development
Good Working Conditions	OR	Recognition

Totals:

Personal Development ____________________

Like-minded Colleagues ____________________

Good Working Conditions ____________________

Stimulating Work ____________________

Achievement ____________________

Fair Pay ____________________

Responsibility ____________________

Recognition ____________________

3.7 One of the major fears I have as a manager is making decisions which affect other people, especially my team members. How can I ease this anxiety?

The key question here from which all else flows is: to what extent can I/should I/must I **involve other team members** in the decision making process? In seeking an answer to that question, remember that, as a general rule, you will feel better about a making a decision if you have shared that process with other people. Not only will you feel less of a personal burden, but your team member(s), through their participation, will have bought into the outcome and will be supportive of it.

Nevertheless, there remain situations where you will have to **make decisions on your own**. Examples would be an emergency fire-fighting scenario where there is no time to consult, implementing corporate decisions whether the team likes them or not and those awkward one to one interviews; e.g. explaining the necessity of making someone redundant.

In fact, you can view the level of involvement of other people in your decision making as a spectrum along which you move to and fro depending on the amount of team involvement which is appropriate in any particular decision making situation. Tannenbaum and Schmidt's **Leadership Continuum** is helpful in this context (see over):

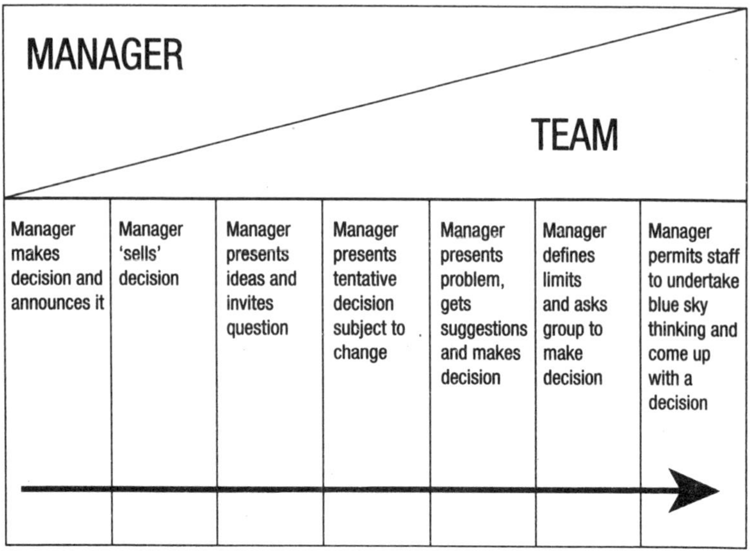

Leadership and Decision Making

The spectrum moves from, for example, those firefighting cases – on the extreme left – where any decision is entirely up to you, to instances where it is vital that the decision is entirely the team's – on the extreme right. An example of this may be the creation of new procedures which the team will use, and where its own understanding of the need and input as to what will and will not work is fundamental to the decision.

In the context of ascertaining whereabouts on the spectrum you should be, you might also take into account the relative **importance of quality and acceptance** of any decision to be made. In other words, is the quality of the decision more important than its overall acceptance by team members? If yes, it is more likely that you will be to the left of the spectrum, either making the decision yourself or with limited team input. Here you won't mind ruffling a few feathers for the sake of getting the decision right. On the other hand, if team commitment to the decision is critical, you may, by being more to the right of the spectrum, go for a compromise position which has been at least democratically arrived at.

All managers have a personal view of where they feel naturally comfortable on the spectrum. Be aware of that position, but do not get stuck in it. Different types of problem solving and decision making require flexibility of approach.

Apart from team input to help you arrive at a decision, there are also a number of **tools and techniques** which you can use to add some useful concrete objectivity to the decision making process. For example:

- *Force field analysis*. The method: draw up two opposing lists, the first containing the reasons why you wish to make the particular decision; the second listing the negative obstacles to making the decision. Ignore the positives and tackle and resolve each negative issue one at a time until you reach the point where only the positives remain – and off you go! This technique has excellent psychological as well as practical positives

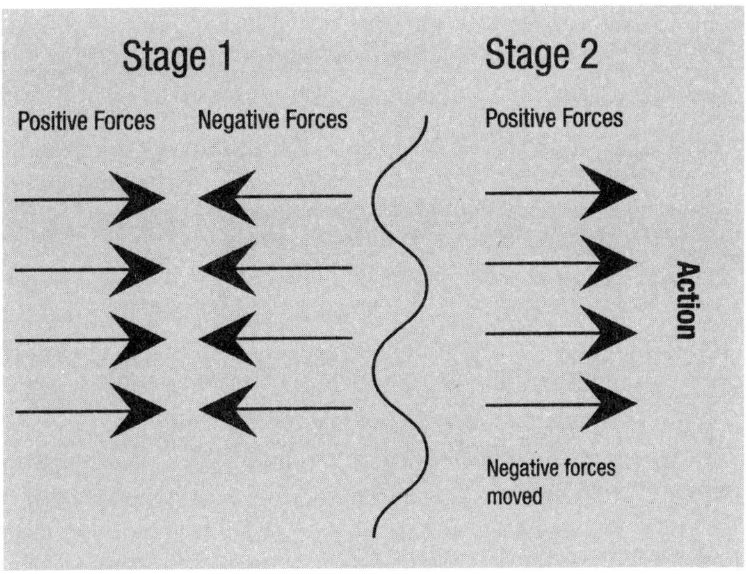

Force Field Analysis

- *The options/criteria matrix.* Here is an example: I wish to travel from London to Glasgow. The following methods of transport are open to me – train, coach, car and plane (if this were a holiday trip, I could add horse, bicycle and walking!). I wish to choose one of these methods by reference to the following criteria – speed, cost, comfort, convenience, timescale and risk of something going wrong. I now draw up a matrix plotting means of transport against the criteria, then score each box out of ten. Finally, I add up the totals for each mode of transport and the one with the highest score 'wins'.

OPTIONS / CRITERIA	TRAIN	COACH	PLANE	CAR
Speed				
Cost				
Comfort				
Convenience				
Timescale				
Risk				

- *Forced pair comparison.* Use this where you need to rank options according to some abstract criterion, e.g. risk, importance. Method: list the options, then compare each with all the others in turn and tick on each occasion which is the more risky, important etc. When finished, add up the ticks to give you the most risky or important option. (For an example of how this works in practice, see question 3.6 above – motivation.)

- *The risk/benefit matrix.* This is a simple four box matrix which plots the risk of failure against the value added of getting the decision right. Using a high/low scale, the options generated appear in the figure below. Act in accordance with where you think your decision should be plotted in the matrix.

	LOW BENEFIT	**HIGH BENEFIT**
HIGH RISK	Leave well alone	Do, but insure against loss
LOW RISK	Why bother?	Do immediately

Summary

Here is a summary of some practical tips and techniques to help you deal with leadership issues:

- Understand the differences between being a manager and being a leader, and what is involved when you slot into each role. Distinguish the role of supervisor, which you might also undertake occasionally.
- Get to grips with the particular tasks that leaders/managers undertake, using as an aid the Adair model of focusing on and integrating the triple elements of task, team and individual.
- Identify the type of team you are leading – line or project – and concentrate on the differing approaches you should take to managing each.
- If you manage a virtual team operating remotely, take into account cultural differences between team members, communicate appropriately (in particular, knowing when face to face contact is essential) and develop specific remote leadership skills.
- Using the Situational Approach model, use different leadership styles – ordering, coaching, delegating and empowering – to

handle more effectively the management requirements of different team situations

- Motivate your team towards ongoing first class performance. Develop a McGregor 'Y' approach, be sensitive to problems at the lower levels of the Maslow pyramid and particularly feed the Herzberg true motivating factors.
- Gain confidence in making decisions by knowing when and how much to involve your team. Use a variety of decision making tools to help you take an objective view of the way you ought to go.

FOUR
Performance management

4.1 My major responsibility for my team members is that of managing their performance not only on a day to day basis but also over extended periods of time. Are there any overarching models or pegs through which I can focus on the big picture of performance management?

The first thing to recognize is that performance management is not solely confined to supporting your team members, although this is the most crucial part of the process. It also includes self-monitoring – how are you doing as a people manager? – considering the performance of the team as a whole and keeping track of the effectiveness of the supporting tools and processes which enable team members to get things done.

Begin by asking yourself how your organization's **culture** views managing performance and what its expectations in this regard are. Is it a people-oriented business or is it more concerned with productive output? What is the relationship between these two ways of looking at its operations? The matrix below describes the effect of this people/production relationship:

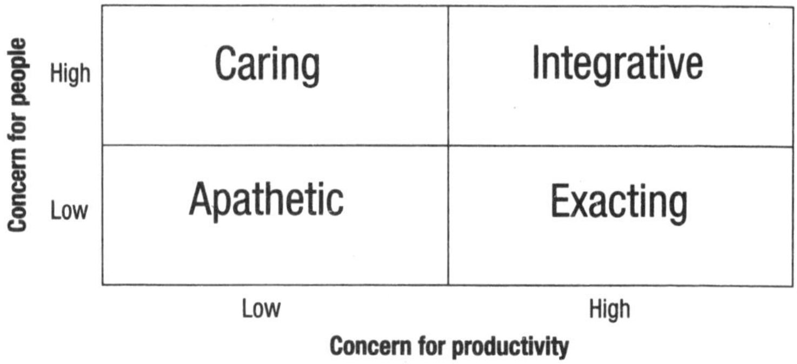

It is unlikely that an apathetic organization will survive for long. The caring and exacting cultures fail to provide a balanced approached to ensuring first rate performance, although it is clear in these cases where the performance management focus should lie. The best culture looks for high performance through an integrative approach which shows concern for both people and productivity.

Having sorted out where your focus should lie, you should then set up a broad based **process** to implement performance management in your team. Here is a general model which describes a performance management cycle:

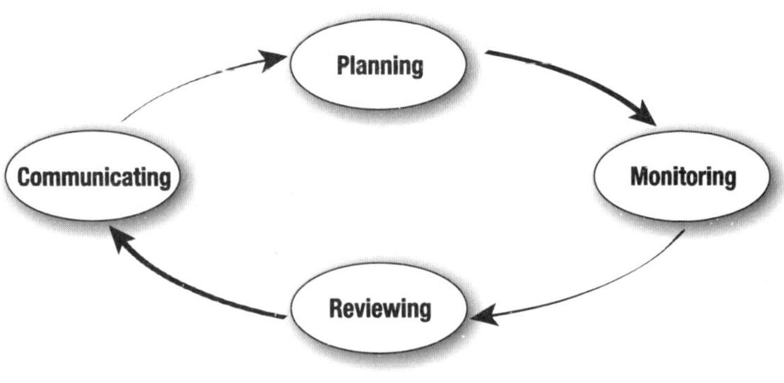

The Performance Management Process

All four of these phases permanently interact, but what should you be concerned about when dealing with any particular phase? Here are some suggestions:

1. **Planning.** You cannot plan for your team unless you understand the big picture. This is an internal communication issue within the organization and involves a successful cascade of information from the top down to you. The Board is concerned with producing an overarching business plan; you are concerned with its implementation within the context of your team's remit. To understand what needs to be done, your manager will explain to you your team's targets in the context of his own strategic targets. In simple terms it works like this:

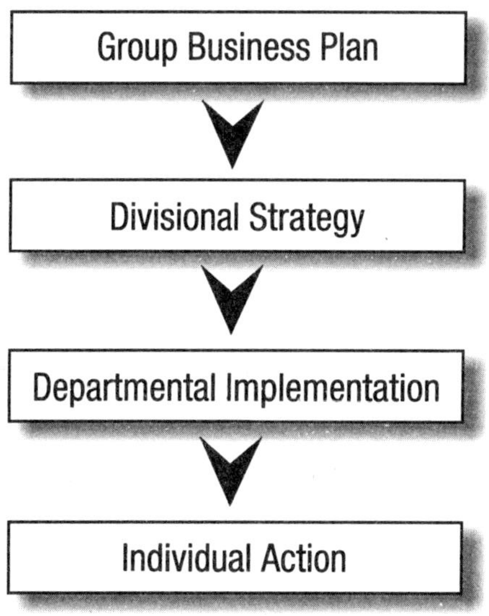

Organizational Information Cascade

You are at the third level here, your manager is at level two and your team members are at level four. Within this framework, you should now set *objectives* for the team. These should be SMART, i.e.:

- Specific – clearly defined
- Measurable – milestones and the end result can be clearly envisaged
- Achievable – can be done subject to defined and agreed cost, quantity and quality parameters
- Realistic – appropriate in the context of the business plan and its implementation
- Timely – being done at the right time and within an agreed timescale

This planning phase is no more important than any other of the four, but may take up a significant amount of your total performance management time.

2. **Monitoring.** You should implement systems for keeping tabs on things as work progresses. This could take the form of a brief weekly team meeting and/or regular or occasional one to one chats with individual team members. You might introduce administrative reporting procedures via spreadsheets or written reports to keep you abreast with what is going on. Ensure that the responsibility for providing the information, in whatever form and whenever required, is effectively delegated to the team. You do not have time to chase it yourself. Your job is to analyze the results. However you decide to monitor, you should be aware that this phase is vital for keeping objectives absolutely on track and raising early warning of existing or future problems.

3. **Reviewing.** The performance management plan must be kept under constant review. Change is endemic in today's working environment and what was clearly SMART six months ago may no longer be so today. Be prepared to make changes whenever necessary, whether to your overall objectives or to the implementation detail.

4. **Communication.** We have already mentioned that this is vital to organizational success at all levels and in all contexts. When managing performance, regular communication is critical with the stakeholders in your team's success. Specifically, this means not only your team members, but your line manager and any other external colleagues or clients whose role has an impact on your team's output.

So, your performance management process involves an ongoing interaction between the above four phases. Juggle them effectively to ensure top team outcomes.

4.2 I understand that the annual appraisal meeting with my individual team members is a part of the performance management system, but why am I continually being told that it is so important? What are the benefits of holding appraisals and why am I so reluctant to do them?

Your performance management system deals with the generalities of managing performance throughout the year. It is concerned with a number of performance issues which relate to you, the team as a whole, the individual members of the team and non-personal support systems. The annual appraisal meeting, on the other hand, is solely concerned with an individual team member's performance (and much more) and is the formal method of assessing past performance and agreeing future action.

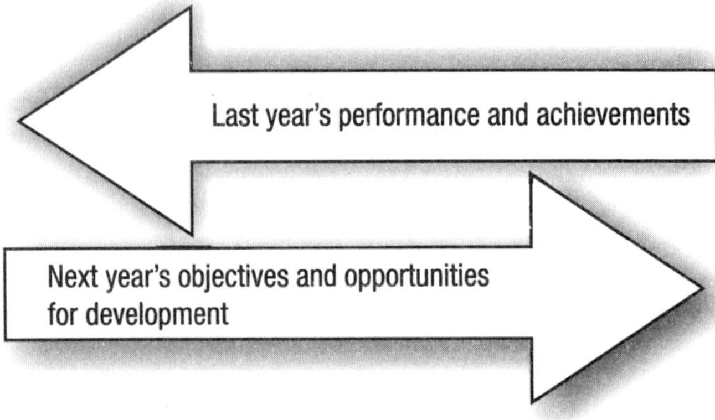

The Appraisal

The appraisal is indeed a vitally important activity because, when all is said and done, *it is the individual contributions of a team's members which produce a team performance, which in turn implements the strategy, which in turn makes the business plan achievable.* The buck therefore stops with each member of staff. Thus:

If there is only one thing you are able to do each year as a people manager, it must be to hold the annual appraisal meetings.

By placing significant importance on the appraisal process, you are sending out to staff a clear message that people are important in your organization and that you recognize that high productivity and success is borne of effectively managing each team member and his performance. It is therefore surprising that managers sometimes fail to realize how crucial these meetings are and put up all sorts of **excuses** for not holding them. Here are some examples:

- *Too tight a window to do them properly.* Most appraisal systems demand that the meetings be concluded within a month, normally towards the end of either the calendar or financial year. I do not have much truck with this moan. As a manager, you know the time is coming. Organize yourself accordingly and if you do nothing else for that month except hold appraisals, so be it. You now know how important the process is. Delegate anything else which needs to be done urgently.

- *Don't like judging people.* As a people manager, you are, or should be, continually making judgements – judgements as to who does what, who is good at this and poor at that, who is ready for promotion, who has managerial potential. If you find this difficult, don't be a people manger!
- *Lack of confidence in follow through.* We have already seen that performance management in general involves monitoring and keeping tabs on how your team members are getting on. Follow through is simply monitoring by reference to the appraisal agreement. Where's the problem?
- *Don't enjoy being negative.* By this you mean criticizing poor performance. Nobody remotely human does. But holding difficult conversations is part of your people management role. You will learn how to handle these interactions and give feedback from later in this chapter (see 4.5 and 4.6). Now put these principles into practice.
- *Formality unnecessary.* Given the linkage between personal performance and business success, you will agree that an annual formal meeting is absolutely appropriate for recording and coordinating performance information so that any potential gaps and needs can be analyzed and plugged. You can be as informal as you like with ongoing monitoring.
- *Process too demanding.* Anything done properly warrants a sound structure and procedure. Your HR team will have produced a system which is right for the organization, and that system must be the same across all departments and workgroups so that the information can be analyzed and used consistently and fairly. You will just have to put up with this process.
- *Time consuming.* Yes it is, and for perfectly solid and important reasons.

- *Pointless paperchase.* We now know that the appraisal process is of course quite the opposite of pointless. As to the paperchase, the HR team will have kept the documentation down to an absolute minimum. They may even have placed standard forms on your IT server to try and turn the appraisal process into a paperless exercise!
- *Involves doing unnecessary things.* Not if you understand what the appraisal process is all about. See the next question for what needs to be done to ensure a first class appraisal meeting and outcome.

So, having dealt with the negatives, here are the **6 key positives** which make appraisal meetings so worthwhile:

1. As we have seen, there is a direct connection between business and individual performance. The appraisal provides the opportunity of *locking business strategy into action at ground level.*

2. If you know what successes each individual has had and the skills they have developed, and also have the realization that some things are not their cup of tea, you can more effectively *plan your department's work* and contribution to the overall organizational effort.

3. Planning involves using and managing your team to best effect. As a result of the knowledge you have gained and agreements reached at the appraisal, you can *utilize your human resources to best advantage* for achieving team objectives.

4. The appraisal chat can be a *substantial motivational tool.* You have the opportunity to discuss and solve problems, allay fears, talk through and resolve frustrations and generally proactively manage the relationship with the team member.

5. How well do you know the members of your team? Use the appraisal to talk about a range of issues of relevance to their performance. Find out what their outside interests are and

see how these match up to the skills they are using for you. In a nutshell, use the opportunity to get to *know your team members better.*

6. Have up to date information on manpower planning, training and skills needs. Having completed the appraisal round, coordinate the information either yourself or with the help of HR. Then draw conclusions from this big picture that will help you with *manpower planning decisions, sorting out skills needs and identifying general training and development requirements.*

4.3 If the appraisal is a vitally important people management activity, what are the key practical points for running a really effective appraisal process?

Depending on the size of your organization, the starting point will probably be your HR department, which will send you a reminder that the appraisal season is about to begin followed by a set of the *documentation* you will need to complete during the course of the process. You should also have copies of last year's appraisals for reference.

You will then need to do the following ahead of the appraisal meeting itself:

1. **Fix times** for meetings. These times should be sufficiently far ahead to allow for proper preparation on both sides – for you and your team members. As a time management exercise, block off days, or even weeks depending on the size of your team, for appraisals only. Include preparation time here – back to back appraisal meetings only for long periods will be exhausting and ultimately counterproductive. Once times are fixed, these become *sacrosanct* in your diary. There is nothing more de-motivating to a team member than to have agreed appraisal times delayed. Action of this sort sends out a clear message that appraisals, and

therefore your team members, are relatively unimportant – and you know by now that this is not the case. Delegate or postpone all other matters.

2. **Not less than one hour**. It is impossible to deal with the appraisal business effectively unless you devote a sufficient amount of time to it. *Sixty minutes is the basic target*. Those people managers who spend less time are not doing the job properly, either because they have not prepared well, or are not interested in their people or are too embarrassed to deal with all the issues effectively or still see the appraisal process as being unimportant. None of these reasons is, of course, an issue for you!

3. **Arrange a location**. This should be *neutral territory* – not your office, nor that of the team member. The appraisal discussion needs to be one where a full and frank exchange of views can take place without let or hindrance, and it is less likely that this will happen if either of you is gaining home advantage. Select a meeting room, preferably away from your departmental base, or consider going outside the office completely. A quiet corner in a local coffee bar tends to be as relaxing an environment as you will find.

4. **Prepare thoroughly**. Here are your key sources of information:

    - Last year's completed appraisal form. This contains the team member's targets and objectives which you will be checking to see if they have been achieved.

    - Any notes you may have made relating to the team member over the last year.

    - Your memory of events where the team member has stood out, whether for good or bad.

    - The views of other more senior colleagues with whom the team member may have worked. Remember to allow enough time for making the requests and receiving the responses, so do this early.

5. **Complete the appraisal documentation**. This is the draft version of your views ahead of the meeting; your team member should be asked to do the same thing. Both of you then turn up to the meeting with a document which forms the basis of your conversation and negotiation.

6. **Produce a structure or agenda for the meeting**. Although the atmosphere and discussion should be as relaxed and informal as possible, you nevertheless need a clear path to follow so that you do not get sidetracked. Depending on the comprehensiveness of the appraisal form, the easiest method is simply to follow this through. Otherwise, create your own agenda and ask the team member is he has anything to add. Remember that it is a joint discussion.

Having completed these tasks, you are now ready for the meeting to commence.

4.4 How should I now run the appraisal meeting itself?

Here are some guidelines which will help you to manage the meeting to best advantage:

- Ideally, there should be *no desk or table to act as a barrier between you*. A couple of armchairs would be good. If there should be a desk or table, don't sit opposite each other. The physical barrier also operates as a psychological barrier. Rather sit at right angles to each other so you are talking round the corner of the table or desk.

- *Shut off the outside world*. Turn off all telephones, close the meeting room door and if possible put up a 'do not disturb' sign.

- Start, as with every influencing conversation, with a *few pleasantries* to put your team member at ease. Many staff find the appraisal a real anxiety generating experience. If you have prepared together properly, much of that will have disappeared already. A brief relaxed chat to put the show on the road will further lessen any anxiety.

- Run briefly through the *agenda* so that both of you get an overview of how the meeting will proceed.

- The discussion itself should then cover four main areas which can be summed up in the mnemonic **RITA**:

  - **R**eflect on last year's performance. Were all targets met? If not, which ones went astray and why? What objectives were particularly successfully achieved and why? What problems occurred along the way and how were they resolved? What generally went less well and why? All this is designed to assess past competence and to reach an agreed conclusion on how that should be rated.

  - **I**mprovement planning. Consider here the general competences of the team member, what he is good at, what not so good at, likes and dislikes plus any other personal factors which will produce better performance within the team as a whole. In effect, do a personal SWOT analysis:

	STRENGTHS What is the team member member good at	**WEAKNESSES** What is the team member less good at
Internal (personal) →		
External (organizational) →	**OPPORTUNITIES** What business and personal possibilities are coming up	**THREATS** What could get in the way of future success

- Targets and objectives for the coming year. The third element of the discussion is what targets and objectives should be set for the coming twelve months. These should reflect a combination of business needs linked to the SWOT analysis, coupled with an element of personal desire to have a go at an interesting project or broaden the base of experience generally. Remember here that the negotiation will include some trade off between business against personal wishes to retain motivation and loyalty. 'This is what you will do' is not a conversational option.
- Actions to be carried out by both parties. These will include not only the targets which the two of you have agreed for the team member, but also any training and development activities he may need, career planning and other related experiences. Since this is an agreement between the two of you, you also must agree how in practice you will support the team member to achieve his goals and objectives through opening doors, making resources available and monitoring progress via your general performance management strategy.

- As you go through the RITA process, *refer to your pre-prepared documentation*. Remember that you will eventually have to agree a final version and this will be negotiated from perhaps two different versions on the table.
- Use your listening skills to full advantage. Ask good open and probing questions, allowing *the team member to do most of the talking*. Encourage and steer his contributions. At the end of the session, you should have discovered a lot more about your team member. He does not need to know too much more about you.

- *Agree the final version* of the appraisal document for formalizing after the meeting.
- End the meeting on a *positive upbeat note* for motivational effect.

The meeting ends and you are nearly there. Now, here are **your final tasks** needed to complete the appraisal process:

- write up the final version of the appraisal documentation;
- send it to the team member for his approval (yes!);
- the team member signs it off;
- you sign it off;
- file a copy where you can readily access it for ongoing performance management;
- send the originals to HR/central filing in accordance with your organization's own system.

You have now concluded a process from which maximum benefits will flow for everyone – your team member, you and, most importantly, your business.

4.5 One of the things which concerns me is how best to give feedback, particularly negative feedback, to a team member in such a way that the team member remains positively motivated. What techniques are there which will help with this issue?

Feedback is something which a people manager has to give to his team regularly. It is part of the ongoing performance management process. You should give it as a follow up to a piece of delegated work, during the annual appraisal meeting, after a coaching session, when generally monitoring progress and ad hoc at any other time when some immediate response to performance is called for – and improved performance will result in improved output.

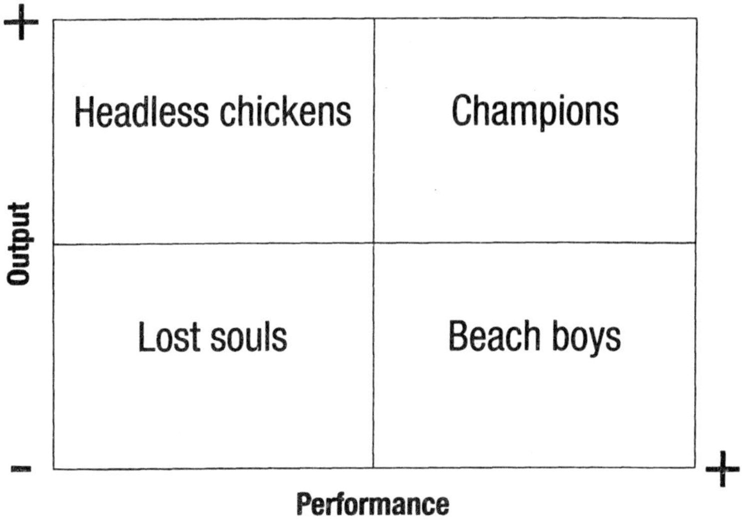

Thus, using the above matrix, the aim of feedback in general terms is to stimulate the beach boys with a dip in cold water, to re-capitate the headless chickens into using some focused thinking and to attempt to resurrect the lost souls. The successful end result will be that all the team members become champions.

Positive feedback is easy, but is often forgotten. Remember to praise and congratulate when a piece of work has been done well. This does wonders for morale and commitment and shows that team members are not being taken for granted.

Negative feedback is far more difficult to get across effectively. The approach you take will depend on the circumstances in which the feedback is being given. Never criticize in an aggressive manner – the hair dryer method – unless the same mistakes are continually being made, a more reasoned and assertive conversation does not appear to have worked, and it appears to you that only short sharp shock will produce a response in the team member. Apart from this, a reasoned conversation is the norm.

Here is why the more reasoned approach should be used on almost every occasion:

CONSTRUCTIVE FEEDBACK	DESTRUCTIVE FEEDBACK
Solves problems	Exacerbates problems
Concentrates on behaviour	Concentrates on attitudes
Strengthens relationships	Damages relationships
Builds trust	Destroys trust
OBJECTIVE	**SUBJECTIVE**

The aim behind giving negative feedback is to get the team member to buy into improved performance, i.e. *own the solution to a problem* which he himself thinks through with your help. The diagram below sets out the key issues you should consider when holding a feedback conversation.

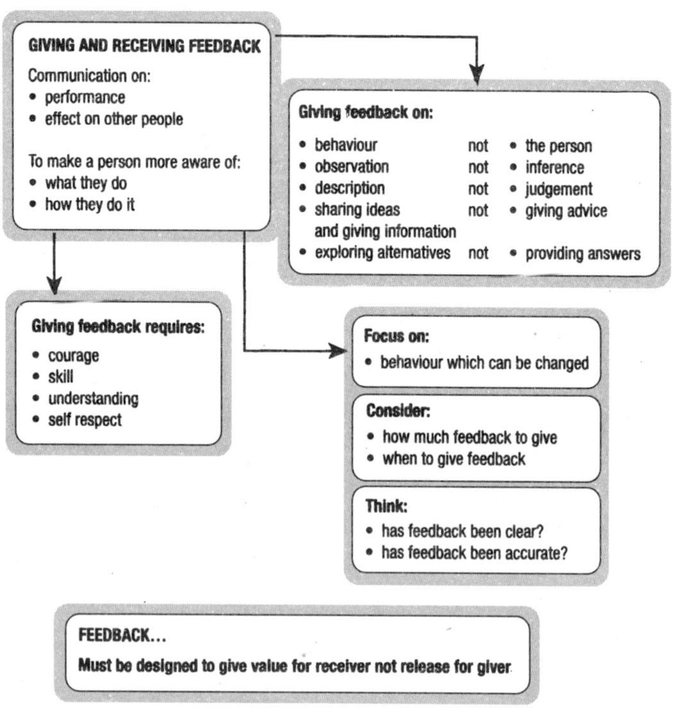

Here is some further explanation of some of the **key points** in the diagram:

- Discuss behaviour and not the individual. If you criticize your team member personally, you have lost the battle before you have even started. The team member will either respond aggressively or meekly and thus lose interest in the possibility of an assertive discussion and positive outcome. Concentrate objectively on what went wrong, e.g.:

  'I saw that there was a problem with the distribution process yesterday. Please talk to me about what happened.' .....rather than.....

  'You made a real mess of the distribution process yesterday. What on earth do you think you were doing?'

- Do not give feedback second hand. Only do so regarding problems of which you have first hand knowledge. Otherwise, your team member may deny that there is an issue and you will have no evidence to support your assertion. In this situation, have a colleague, who directly witnessed what occurred, present at the start of the conversation to verify the facts. He can then leave and the two of you continue in private with sorting things out.

- Describe the resulting problem objectively rather than pass judgement on it. So:

  'The consequence of the distribution problem was unsatisfactory in that we ended up with an irate customer. Do you agree?' .....is better than...

  'I thought that the angry customer we had as a result of the distribution problem was a totally unacceptable consequence.'

- In seeking a solution to the problem, have a discussion that shares ideas and explores alternative possible courses of action. Do not give advice (unless expressly asked for) or provide answers. Remember that you are looking for the team member to come up with a workable solution that he then owns.

- In determining how 'heavy' the feedback should be, consider the seriousness of the problem, the frequency of its occurrence and the receptiveness of the team member. There is no point being too firm over what is a relatively minor issue, or in going on at length about a major one when a light touch of the rudder would ensure the appropriate change of course.

So, the aim is to get the team member *to understand the issue and to suggest a solution that, when agreed, belongs to him*. This will ensure that the feedback problem does not occur again and that the team member remains focused and committed to his job and improving its execution.

Here is a **three stage model** which could act as structure around which your feedback conversation might revolve. Notice that it is predicated on questions so that the team member has to do all the creative thinking and responding, and also that the chat begins with the good news:

- *Stage 1* – What went well for you [in the project you have just concluded]?
- *Stage 2* – What did not go quite so well and why?
- *Stage 3* – How would you suggest these issues are tackled differently so as to improve things on the next occasion?

Note that these questions are simply conversation starters. You may not agree with the responses, in which case you will need to point out any problems, ask further probing questions or ask for the other side's opinion on an alternative approach which you suggest. However the conversation progresses, you are aiming for a win-win outcome with which the team member is happy, so that he walks out of your door motivated and owning the route to future progress.

4.6 A feedback or other potentially difficult conversation is fine if it all goes well, but what should one do if things turn nasty and there is a real conflict through difference of opinion?

There is nothing more awkward, tiring and stressful for a people manager than to experience conflict within his team. Whatever the cause of the difference of opinion and whether the opposing views have validity or not, it is critical that you bring back peace and harmony to the workplace as quickly as possible. There are two different scenarios which might occur here either independently or in combination.

The first is where the other side is really **upset and has a verbal 'go'** at you. Not only is this quite frightening in its own right – any emotional outburst is unsettling – but you may be wondering if it might escalate to something physical.

Should you ever be faced with this situation, follow this four point plan of action:

- *Allow the other side to blow himself out.* Do not interrupt but be prepared to take the outburst until the emotional energy starts to drain away. What is happening is that his geyser has blown and the pent up tension is now using anger as its means of dissipation. Under no circumstances interrupt at this stage. Phrases like 'Calm down', or even 'I understand', will simply make matters worse. Stay silent.

- Once the tension in the situation has started to ebb (and it will be a matter of judgment for you when that moment has arrived), *say something neutral* such as: 'I realize that you clearly have an issue here. Shall we talk about it further now (in my office)?' If you have picked the right moment, the other side will be thinking reasonably rationally by this time and will probably agree. If he does not, fix a later time to which he will agree.

- Once things have calmed down, ask your team member to *start at the beginning and explain again* what the problem is. On this occasion you should get a coherent story rather than one that may have been difficult to follow when emotions were high.
- Once the issues are clear, treat the *search for a solution* rather like a feedback session. Ask questions that elicit positive answers and ideas for resolving the problem from the other side, such as:
  - *'I realize that you are angry with the way I dealt with [the situation]. How do you think I might handle things better next time?'...or...*
  - *'I understand that there was a real problem for you with the [outcome of that meeting]. What do you suggest we might do to make things work for you?'*
  - As with feedback discussions, the answers you are given may not stack up to a viable solution so be prepared to *discuss modifications or alternatives* until you reach an outcome acceptable to both of you.

If you can manage to handle this type of difficult situation in the way suggested, i.e. coolly and calmly in the face of anger, it will surprise you how much respect and credibility this adds to you managerial stock, not only within the team as a whole but also from your erstwhile protagonist.

The second scenario which might cause you difficulty is where you have a **genuine difference of opinion with someone** and there appears to be an impasse to progress and resolution of the problem.

How this manifests itself in practice depends on how assertive each side is in sticking to its point of view set against how willing both are to cooperate with each other in order to sort things out. The matrix below sets out the resulting scenarios.

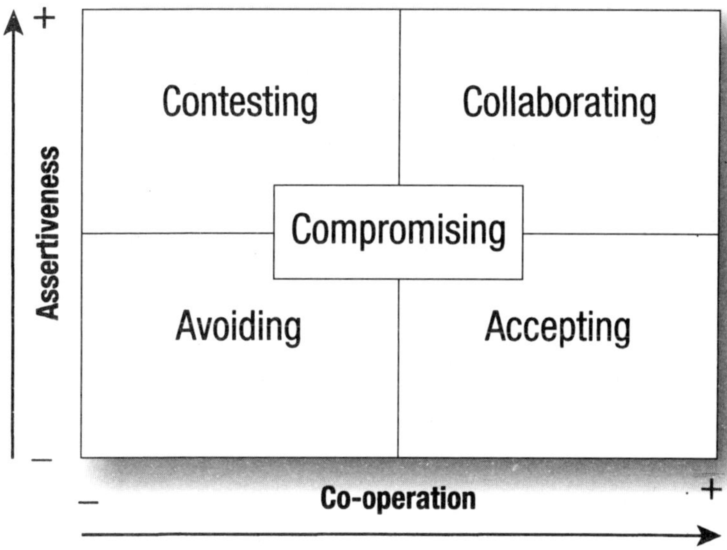

The Five Conflict Handling Modes

There are five situations to consider:

1. Low assertiveness/low cooperation. This is one of the positions you are likely to be in at the start. Both of you are *avoiding* the issue. You think it better to ignore the problem and hope it goes away. Clearly, no progress will ever be made if you continue to sit in this box.

2. High assertiveness/low cooperation. Here is what may possibly be the second phase of conflict development where the issue is now out on the table, but neither of you is willing to give an inch. Both positions are clearly stated but you are entrenched in your differences and in *contesting* mode. Again, there will be no further progress if there is no movement out of this box.

3. Low assertiveness/high cooperation. This scenario envisages a recognition that a problem exists and that there is a need

to resolve it, but neither side is really willing to face up to the realities of the situation, opting for any solution so long as they can then forget about things and get on again as if nothing had ever happened. This is the *accepting* box, and whilst there may be short term merit here in things moving forward in some sort of way, it is most likely that the issue has in reality simply been swept under the carpet and that it will crawl out again to cause further trouble at a later date.

4. High assertiveness/high cooperation. Here is the ideal position to be in for sorting the problem out. Both sides are *collaborating* to produce the optimum solution. They are initially maintaining their positions, but, through argument, influencing and negotiation are prepared to move towards an outcome which satisfies everyone, being based on a solid foundation of extensive and positive discussion.

5. Right in the middle of the matrix is the fifth position of *compromise*. Here, the assertiveness/cooperation relationship is in limbo with both sides being neither assertive enough nor sufficiently willing to cooperate to reach a solid and sensible settlement. A compromise may well be workable, but because it is usually neither one thing nor the other, it satisfies nobody and is generally a fudge driven by timescales and, often, politics. Compromises are never lasting solutions and will need to be revisited at some stage.

So, in these difficult situations, keep a cool head and work toward a collaborative solution to the problem. That way, everyone wins in the end.

Summary

Here is a summary of some practical tips and techniques to help you deal with performance management issues:

- Make sure that your performance management activities do not concentrate solely on your team. Include yourself and other supporting processes. Work alongside the organization's culture in managing performance.
- Use effectively the four elements of the performance management cycle – plan, monitor, review and communicate.
- Understand the critical importance of the formal appraisal for your team members. Appreciate and resist any arguments for not holding appraisal meetings.
- Set up and follow a comprehensive procedure for running the appraisals. Take into account location and timing, plan thoroughly and maximize the use of any standard appraisal documentation.
- Structure and run the appraisal meeting itself following an agenda. Use the RITA approach to the discussion. Ask incisive questions and listen proactively. The appraisee should do most of the talking.
- Learn to give solid positive feedback. Don't forget to praise, and develop the techniques for giving a negative message whilst retaining your team member's commitment and motivation.
- When confronted with anger, allow the emotion to ebb away before entering into a discussion aimed at solving the problem. When there is a difference of opinion with a colleague, use the conflict handling modes model to help move you both towards a win-win solution.

FIVE
Organizational skills for managers

5.1 Now that I have a team of people to lead and manage as well as myself, it becomes much more important that team operations are well organized. This has never been easy for me. How can I improve my organizational abilities?

The effectiveness and efficiency with which you team functions is, to a large extent, down to the way you manage yourself. This involves incorporating practical organizational skills into your working life to support the key leadership attributes of vision, communication, motivation and achieving success.

The critical activity around which all else revolves is **planning**. Without planning, you will have no idea what you should be doing or when it needs to be done. You will simply react in an unstructured way on a day to day basis to whatever turns up. Here are some of the major advantages of planning:

- It is a proactive example of leadership activity – you are moving forward your vision
- It gives you a comprehensive overview of your team's aims and tasks that need to be done
- It enables you to organize the efficient use of team resources
- You gain confidence and a sense of control over your work commitments
- By thinking ahead, you better understand the tasks and problems that require your attention

- You are better able to monitor more the performance of both yourself and your team
- Planning is a very effective de-stressor!

You must therefore proactively plan everything, from the big picture objectives which your team is seeking to achieve to the execution of the detail by your team members, to ensure that those objectives happen.

Here is a list of basic matters for which you must plan:

- Your team members – have you recruited/do you have in place the right team membership?
- The work/tasks that the team needs to accomplish
- The allocation of tasks to the most appropriate team members
- The timescales within which things must happen – these last three items can be successfully monitored by the use of GANNT charts
- The budgets needed to achieve objectives and how they will be managed
- The physical resources that the team needs at any given time.

Planning comes more naturally and easily to some managers than others. Those of you with a J in your Myers Briggs profile will find the planning process stimulating and a normal element of managerial life; those with a P in their profile will find it tedious and stressful. Myers Briggs Ps must therefore work much harder to ensure that their teams' future activities are effectively mapped out (see 2.2 above).

Case study

Fred is a very bright and creative IT expert. He has held a number of leading IT positions in organizations which are household names. He has, however, held each of these positions for a relatively short period of time. This is because he was brought in on each occasion to add significant technical value, but as a Myers Briggs P and DISC I was unable to plan effectively for his teams which resulted in major frustration and demotivation. On one occasion, he developed a project strategy with the team which went off to get on and prepare things, and then, the day before the project was due to go live, changed his mind on a major issue with the result that the weeks of preparatory work done by the team proved useless. Fred left the organization shortly after this incident. Fred is now a leading international IT consultant and has found his true metier free of people management responsibilities.

Having said all this, and hopefully done a hard sell to you on the need for planning, the best laid plans go wrong or require modification/fine tuning from time to time. This is because your team and what it does is not acting in isolation but is subject to the impact of what goes on elsewhere, both within the organization and outside it. Plans therefore need to be **monitored** and approached with a degree of **flexibility**. Otherwise, the rigidity of a tunnel vision approach towards the plan will mean it will end in disaster. The fact that plans may, and probably will, have to change over a period of time does not however invalidate the need to plan. You can see from the graph below (which plots the life of a years plan from January to December) that monitoring and change has not only varied the track along which the original plan was supposed to travel, but, in an alternative scenario, may have ended up at a different destination (Z) from that originally targeted (Y). Nevertheless, the need for a structure arising from an ongoing yet flexible plan remains an essential organizational tool.

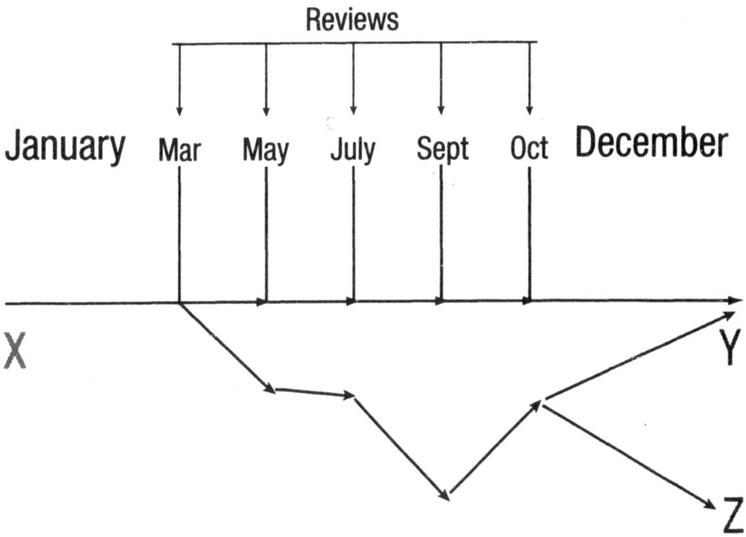

The Planning Process

5.2 I am not particularly good at organizing my own working practices. What tips and techniques should I use to help show the team that I can manage my own as well as their work contributions?

You, as a people manager, are part of the team plan you have put together and as such must, alongside your team members, organize yourself to play your full and effective part in getting things done efficiently.

Personal organization is a huge topic in its own right, but in essence it comes down to an **efficient and effective use of time**. That means that you must organize your working day in such a way that you maximize your output and at the same time do the right tasks at the right time. As their manager, your team will be looking to you for a self-organizational lead.

Here are three key tips and techniques that you should employ:

1. Set up a **'to-do' list** and **prioritize** the tasks on it.

   Most of us produce to-do lists quite readily. What we don't necessarily do is use the list to ensure maximum value added for our organization and ourselves by prioritizing it effectively. One of the standard ways of categorizing tasks is to differentiate between those which are *urgent* and those which are *important*. Urgent tasks are ones which are subject to a tight timescale for completion, usually no more than 48 hours. Important task are ones which directly impact on the achievement of your personal, team and organizational objectives and thus add value through the work that you are specifically employed to undertake. Using this differentiation, it is now possible to produce a four box matrix which plots the level of urgency against the level of importance as below.

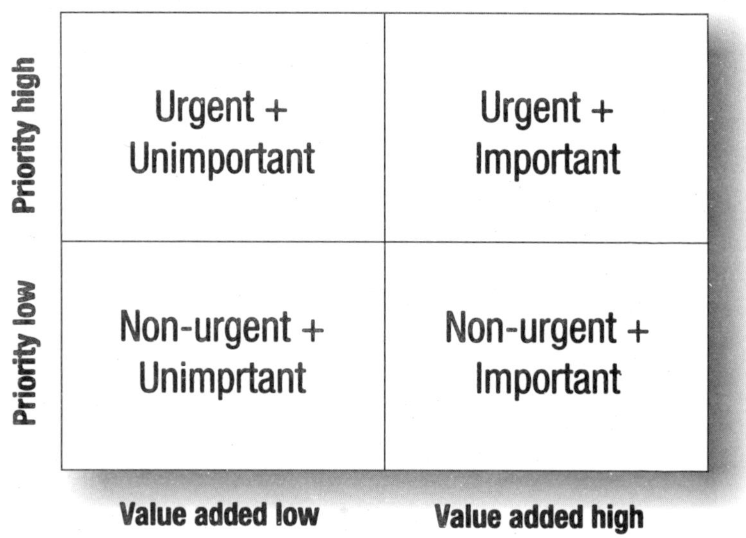

Urgent v Important

Now, using your own judgement (it is *your* to-do list), slot the tasks on your to-do list into the appropriate boxes. The number of tasks in each box may well differ – some boxes will be more demanding than others, but that's fine. Next, prioritize by numbering the tasks in each box separately. Subject to the order in which you work through the boxes (see below), you now have a precise order for getting your work done.

Just in case you think all this is too rigid, ensure that flexibility is built into the system in the following three ways:

- Move tasks around the boxes and/or renumber as they become more or less urgent/important
- Be prepared for new tasks to appear. When they do, slot them in to the appropriate box and renumber depending on where the new tasks fit within the current prioritization list. Thus, there is never any need to panic!
- We do not work in hermetically sealed pods cut off from the rest of the human race, let alone our organizational colleagues. Everyone has their own prioritized to-do list. Be prepared to deviate from your strict task order where a colleague needs your help more urgently than you might otherwise have been prepared to give it.

2. Use **prime time** for critical work

   We all work on personal biological clocks, which mean that each of us is more or less effective at different times of the day. Prime time is that time at which we are most effective. The simplest way to work with this principle is to ask yourself whether you work better earlier in the day or later in the day. If the former, you are a *lark*; if the latter, you are an *owl*.

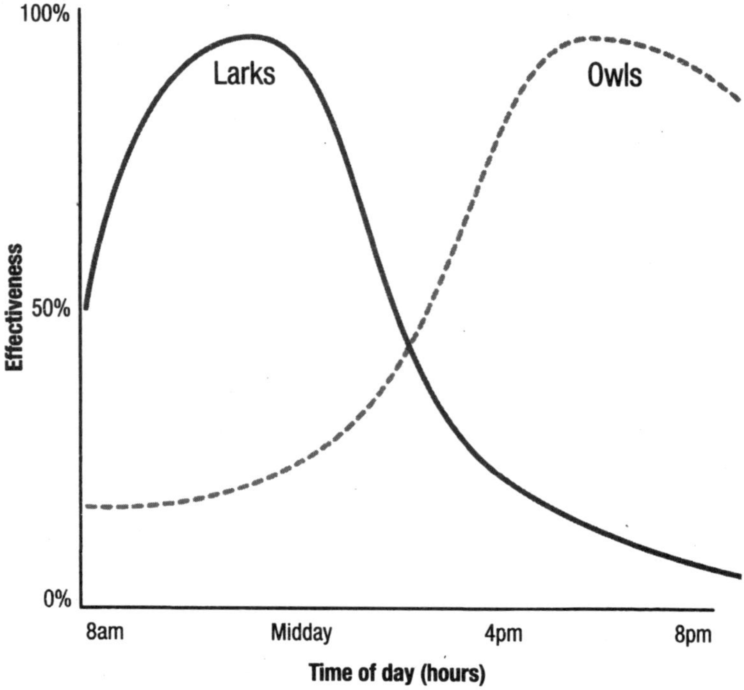

Prime Time

Returning to our four box matrix, the top two boxes (both urgent) should probably be completed today – or tomorrow at the latest. Using your prime time, do the urgent and important tasks at your most effective time of the day. Do the urgent but unimportant when you are less effective. So larks will probably start with the urgent and important, whereas owls will begin with the urgent but unimportant that normally require less real thinking capabilities to execute.

One final point. Most of us are less than proficient immediately after lunch. Counter this by having a light lunch only and getting some fresh air, preferably with a short walk as exercise.

3. Maximize the use of your **diary**

   Diaries enable you to structure your time. As a team leader, you will be busy with various types of meeting at various locations, and you will fail to keep track of these demands on your time if you do not use an appropriate diary system.

   Furthermore, diaries should not be used simply for appointments. When planning your day, block off slots in which to make serious progress on the important tasks. If you do not, you will find yourself frittering away precious time on trivialities.

   Here are a few tips on diaries:

   - *Never run two diaries.* Some people have one for work and one for social activities. This is a recipe for chaos. Life, particularly as you progress in your career, becomes a seamless interactive web of work and social demands. Not only is this because of the increasing level of managerial work commitments which fail to fit into a nine to five pattern, but also, as organizations become more flexible and concern themselves only with their people achieving personal output targets rather than checking on their time inputs, you will have greater freedom to choose which hours you work whilst retaining a sensible work/life balance.

   - *Select a system which works for you.* Most of us are locked in to a computerized diary at work – usually Outlook – which we are compelled to use so that features such as meeting wizards can work effectively. If so, consider acquiring a PDA to enable you to keep in touch with what is going on when you are away from your desk. The alternative is to print out the relevant Outlook pages which is both tedious and of limited use.

   - If you are still able to use a *paper diary system,* choose one which is sufficiently *sophisticated* for your needs as a people manager. A Boy Scout's top pocket job with a pencil down the spine is not appropriate. An A5 or larger desk diary may be all right although a little awkward to carry about. The best bet is a filofax or similar dedicated time management system. The disadvantage, of course, of all paper diaries is that if they go missing, then all is, literally, lost. In this situation, the technology is manifestly superior. A lost PDA is replaceable and its information immediately redownloadable from your PC.

5.3 Despite being well organized, I find that I am prone to a variety of interruptions which prevent me from getting on with my to-do list. How should I tackle these interruptions?

Interruptions are a fact of life. We cannot avoid them but we can manage them so that the adverse effect that they have on our working day is reduced to a minimum. As a people manager, you are more prone than most to being interrupted by your team members. You may decide to see these interruptions as inevitable and build the time they take into your standard working day. But even so, there are ways of doing this in a structured manner (see below).

Interruptions take a variety of forms. They can be defined as anything which gets in the way of your plan or task concentration – ranging from a false fire alarm through a computer system failure to a phone call about some domestic issue from your partner. Here are some of the most common forms of interruption and some suggestions for dealing with them. Notice that most of those mentioned below contain a self-induced element. Not all interruptions are solely caused by external factors.

1. **People interruptions**. As mentioned above, this is likely to be a problem for you since your team members need access from time to time to discuss various issues where your input

is essential. Rather then dealing with these ad hoc, consider blocking off a slot each day lasting, say, an hour and preferably at the same time each day. Use this slot for holding a 'clinic' when team members know that this is their time and can approach you with whatever issues require your input. By using this sort of structure, only emergency matters should necessitate an interruption at any other time. Another tip here is to make sure your delegation skills are up to speed (see below). Some interruptions may be caused by poor coaching or an ineffective briefing process when discussing the delegated job with your team member.

Apart from this team issue, here are some general tips for keeping unwanted people at bay:

- Operate a *closed door policy*. If you have your own office, this is self-explanatory – closed means I'm busy; open means I'm available. In an open office environment, things are more difficult to control. Some interesting ideas include hanging a 'do not disturb' notice across your back or positioning red or green flags on your VDU. Devise a policy which works for you. You may receive some leg pulling to start with but eventually your system will be respected.
- *Be assertive*. This is essential where the topic of conversation is not work related. Often, we feel churlish if we brush someone off with a grunt, particularly if it is a close colleague. Rather, say pleasantly but firmly that you are busy and, 'no', this is not the time to discuss last night's football results, but how about a drink after work or let's have lunch to talk about our common outside interests.
- *Book appointments*. When interrupted on a work related matter other than an emergency, respond immediately with a comment that you are currently busy but (having referred to your diary) would three o'clock this after-

noon be ok for a chat? This way, you can keep control of your to-do list.

- *Body language*. Often, the person interrupting you is standing over you whilst you are seated. This puts you at physical and consequently psychological disadvantage. Stand up so that you are able to make eye contact on equal terms. This way, you are able to express your own sense of urgency and also make the person interrupting slightly uneasy at the positive move you have made to cut short the conversation.

2. **Incoming Emails**. Most people seem to have an apparently irresistible urge to read an email as soon as it arrives. This urge must be resisted. Every email which is opened as an instinctive reaction to its appearance in the inbox cuts across your thought process and interrupts your concentration level for the task your were carrying out. This mental leaping about between tasks and the effort it takes to refocus on what you were doing beforehand is a serious waste of time.

   Here are some tips for fighting email reading addiction:

   - *Turn off all dialogue boxes and sound* which inform you of an email's arrival. You cannot be tempted by what you do not know exists.

   - Slot into your day a number of *brief occasions when you will check your inbox*. Five may be about right – first thing, mid morning, lunchtime, mid afternoon and close of play.

   - *Read the new emails at that time and treat them as tasks,* prioritizing your full response using your prioritization system. The sender of non-urgent emails which are nevertheless important should be given a brief 'holding' response but no more at that time. All non-urgent and unimportant emails should be deleted.

- *Use the filing possibilities of your email system to their full potential*. In particular, set up files for different projects, clients, tasks etc, and also create a pending file into which emails still requiring action can be temporarily placed. The aim is always to have an empty inbox once you've done your check.

If you institute a process something like the above, you will quickly find that email becomes your servant rather than your master. Remember that the longest anyone will have to wait for an urgent and important email to be dealt with is one and a half hours if they are unlucky. Think to yourself that this is a lot less than their waiting time would be if you were in an all day meeting or out on an external visit.

3. **Incoming telephone calls**. In many ways, the problems here are similar to emails. There is an instinctive reaction in us to answer the phone when it rings and that interruption has the same knock on effect as reading an email. However, there is often one important difference here and that is that it may be company policy for employees to answer all incoming calls as they happen. If this is the case, you clearly must abide by the policy, but recognize that the policy is validating one of the most common and awkward forms of interruption.

   Apart from this, why not treat telephone calls in the same way as emails? Maximize your use of voicemail. Turn the ringer off and make sure that your message is permanently up to date and makes it clear that you will respond as soon as possible. Then operate the 'five times a day' and prioritization principles. You will find that your concentration levels, and thus the quality of your work, will increase dramatically if you can free yourself in this way from the phone for certain periods of time.

   But remember again the principle of flexibility here. With both the telephone and email, make occasional space to be immediately available, e.g. when doing the urgent but unimportant tasks. The strategy to cut yourself off for a while is to enable you to execute effectively your important value added work.

4. **Untidiness**. This refers to clutter on your desk/workstation and in particular a mess of disorganized paperwork. If your desk is invisible because of the amount of documentation of one sort or another on it, then there are three negative consequences:

   - You are wasting time when having to plough through the morass to come up with particular bits of paper needed at any particular moment.
   - You are setting a disorganized example to your team who may take the view that you are consequently not totally in control of things.
   - If you go on holiday or are run over by a bus, it is unfair on colleagues who have to fight their way across your desk to find out what is going on, when and for whom.

   If this is a problem for you, here are **three key tips** to improve things:

   - *Institute the principle of the 4 Ds.* Every piece of paper that comes across your desk should be dealt with in one of four ways – DO (action immediately); DEFER (can only be done when other things happen later); DELEGATE (pass it to a member of your team to do); DUMP (into the waste paper bin). Using this tip, your desk becomes simply a transition zone – paper is always on its way elsewhere.
   - For the DEFER items, *create a brought forward file.* This should have sufficient pockets for each day of the month and number them as such. Then slot the deferred piece of paper into the date that you will next require it. Take

out the papers each morning which are relevant to today's date, and these originally deferred items immediately become a DO, DELEGATE or DUMP and things continue to move on.

- Quite apart from the brought forward file, *create a filing system that works for you*. It should be clear and simple. Complex filing systems create misery, since eventually you will waste even more time wondering where a particular piece of paper should go. But a straightforward filing system saves time, allowing you to retrieve paper fast whilst retaining a clear desk.

One factor that is increasingly assisting with overcoming the paper problem is that, as technology becomes ever more sophisticated, we move even closer to the so-called paperless office. For example, the fax is now at the very least obsolescent having been replaced by email attachments. This makes for less clutter and easier paper filing, but makes computerized filing ever more important.

5. **Procrastination**. A major time waster is the self-induced interruption we call procrastination. This occurs when something which should be done at a particular time is deferred without good reason. Generally, that less than good reason involves fear on your part that you will fail at the task, or that potential feedback you are about to receive will be negative, or that you just don't feel like doing that particular job today. In brief, procrastination is caused by a combination of lack of self-confidence and laziness. As a people manager, you should by now have got over these negative work attitudes. Your team will notice them and that will have an adverse effect on morale.

Consider the following statements:

- *I invent reasons and look for excuses for not acting on a tough problem*
- *There are too many interruptions and crises that interfere with my achieving important tasks*
- *I avoid assertive answers when pressed for an unpleasant decision*
- *I delegate unpleasant assignments which should really be up to me*
- *I'm too tired/anxious to do the difficult tasks that face me*

These are a mere handful of procrastination situations. If any of these ring a bell, you have at least some sort of a problem.

How should you deal with procrastination? The simple answer is to develop your capacity for willpower. More practically, plan effectively and make sure you do not deviate unnecessarily from your prioritized to-do list. Also, try jumping in the deep end to kick start something difficult. That way, the task automatically starts to run and you must run with it if you are not to look foolish or incompetent. Psychologically, develop a healthy sense of guilt – but not so deep that you become immobilized. And don't forget that nothing ever turns out to be quite as bad as your fertile imagination would have you believe. When all is said and done, *just get on with it!*

5.4 Like all managers, I need to meet with my team members to discuss issues relevant to our work, gain their views and make decisions. I am not entirely clear about the organizational and administrative issues involved. What should I bear in mind when setting up such meetings and how can I manage them more efficiently and effectively?

Meetings are said by many to be the curse of business life. They need not be, but meeting management skills are singularly lacking in most managers and this causes major problems. The worst of these problems are holding unnecessary meetings and hanging around far too long in those which are necessary. Meetings are potentially a big time waster. The public sector, where meetings are often constitutionally essential under a formal committee structure, is invariably the worst offender. The end result of a meeting should be a decision or series of decisions, and the democratic process to this end can be achieved quite happily in as short a period of time as is reasonably possible.

Here are the key questions you should ask yourself ahead of a meeting:

1. Do you need a meeting in the first place?

Meetings should be held only where a democratic decision from that meeting is needed on a particular issue or set of issues.

To this principle there are three exceptions. Firstly, where comprehensive information from those attending is a critical basis for decision making by you as manager outside the meeting, or for taking a formal decision in another forum, and the meeting is the most efficient vehicle for obtaining that information. Secondly, where the meeting is part of an information cascade process from you (e.g. project briefing) or senior management (eg major strategic issue), and the plenary session is an important element in ensuring group cohesion through personal contact and the ability to ask and have answered pressing questions. Thirdly, you should hold your own team meeting regularly as a trust building and interpersonal bonding exercise at the same time each week (15 minutes only on average), even if there is nothing pressing to discuss (in which case five minutes maximum).

If none of these criteria exists, don't hold a meeting, but rather consider other forms of communication, particularly for purely imparting information. Emails or documents sent as email attachments serve this purpose perfectly well.

2. Do you have clear objectives and projected outcomes for the meeting?

Always think through in general terms what the reason is for having the meeting in the first place and what outcomes you would like to see emerging from it. If there are several disparate matters to deal with, make sure you have views on them all. As chair, you have significant power to influence and persuade towards your own wishes. Planning how you would wish the meeting to go is an essential and valuable time investment.

3. Have you invited the right people to the meeting?

The key issue here is to invite only those who have a contribution to make to the matters under discussion (exception: your weekly team get-together when the purpose of the session has an additional psychological slant to it). Having people sitting around with no interest whatsoever in the proceedings is a serious waste of their valuable time. Furthermore, people who do need to be present may have a direct interest in and input to part of the meeting only. Be prepared here for these people to come and go as need dictates. Do not manifest a dictatorial sense of control by requiring the presence of all those attending all of the time where this is clearly unnecessary. Others who should be invited are those who may be supportive of you in handling a difficult discussion where opposition could be fierce. Tactical and political support from a big gun or two, whose only role is to provide that support, may sometimes be both helpful and necessary.

4. Have you produced an agenda?

Always create an agenda, even for those short team meetings where there may be only one topic for discussion. The agenda lets those attending know what the meeting will be all about and will confirm whether their presence will be helpful or not. Here are some tips for drawing up an agenda:

- *Ask participants* if they have anything they wish to discuss over and above your own items. Give people a sensible amount of time to respond but create a deadline for submissions

- *Order the items* according to importance and urgency. This way, if time does run out ahead of completion of all agenda business, it will be the less critical matters that are held over. Equally, this approach is more likely to free up those who do not need to be present for the whole meeting at the earliest opportunity

- *Allocate items* to individual participants to lead, so that there is always one person responsible for stimulating discussion on each item

- *Never add AOB* at the end of the agenda. This usually breeds prolonged and unnecessary discussion of trivia. Once the agenda deadline has closed, only talk about additional issues on the day if they have become really urgent and important in the interim

- *If any supporting documentation* is needed to help with discussion of any particular item, ensure that these papers are acquired and attached. Alternatively, indicate what other pre-meeting activity might be helpful to save time

- *Distribute* the agenda as far ahead of the meeting as possible in order to give those attending time to read, digest and marshal their thoughts for presentation. This way, those who turn up without having prepared themselves effectively have only their own time management shortcomings to blame

5. Have you clearly set out the length of the meeting?

There is nothing worse than an open-ended meeting. Everyone lists a start time on their agenda, but how many times have you seen a finish time? Lack of a finish time is a recipe for bad meetings management.

When the agenda is finalized, *assess how long the meeting is likely to run*. Add this to the start time and publicize on the agenda the resulting end time as the point at which the meeting will finish. This allows those attending to plan the remainder of their day without the anxiety of a potentially never ending discussion (or worse still, waffle).

Better still, *assess the likely length of discussion of each agenda item* and add timings to these. This will focus the mind wonderfully on getting the business done, and if your assessments have been (should have been) realistic, guillotine discussion at the end of the allotted time (making a swift decision as to 'next steps' on the back of a perfectly adequate and comprehensive exchange of views) and move on.

Be tough on timings. Start promptly. You can wait for ever for latecomers, and never backtrack for these people, especially if they haven't apologized ahead of the meeting for their late appearance. Then call a halt at the designated end time, leaving outstanding matters, if any, over to the next occasion.

6. Have you chosen the optimum location for the meeting?

Here are some points to bear in mind when considering the location of your meeting:

- In the case of internal meetings, *pick a site which is as central as possible* if the meeting is an interdepartmental project meeting. This way, everyone has the lowest average distance to travel. For departmental meetings, stay within the department.

- Where external people will be present – customers, advisors, etc – consider whether *a home, away or neutral territory* is the best location. In negotiating terms, it is often, as with sport, much more comfortable to be operating on home soil.
- *Avoid excessive opportunities for nourishment* in your meetings. Varieties of drinks and foodstuffs simply add to an unwanted sense of comfort, and detract from the mental focus that is required for the business in hand. If anything, provide water only.
- Some organizations now have *chairless meeting rooms.* Participants stand at a circular 'breakfast bar' on which papers can be rested and notes written. The ultimate discomfort of standing in this way for any significant length of time tends to move the meeting rapidly (and successfully) towards a speedy conclusion.

Here is an example of a structured agenda:

MEETING OF THE [MARKETING] DEPARTMENT				
Date: Tuesday 31 Jan 06		Time: 2.00pm	Duration: 2 hours	
Location: Room G5 – Landfill site				
AGENDA				
Item no	Item	Duration	Proposer	Pre-research
1.	XYZ	45 mins	Jo Bloggs	Read....
2.	ABC	30 mins	Fred Smith	None
3.	FGH	20 mins	Jane Green	Think through
4.	KLM	15 mins	Sue Brown	Read...
5.	PQR	10 mins	Jim White	None

7. Will you have all the relevant people/paperwork in front of you at the meeting?

You will have done your best to invite all those who need to be present at the meeting and have attached as much relevant documentation to the agenda as was possible at the time. Nevertheless, it remains true that there is always some person whose input is critical to the meeting who cannot make it at the last minute and whose absence throws the whole timetable for decision making into jeopardy. Again, there are occasions when participants forget to bring files or other crucial documentation for reference purposes which wastes significant time whilst the problem is sorted out.

These annoyances need to be addressed as calmly as possible. See if the absentee, for example, has a fully briefed a number two who can take over and provide the necessary input for him. Remind all participants via the agenda to bring all supporting documentation which is their responsibility, and always have spare sets of agenda papers to hand.

When all is said and done meetings do sometimes needs to be postponed, but this should be a last resort.

8. Have you planned to record effectively the outcome of the meeting and/or produce appropriate minutes?

The key point about minutes is that they **should be brief**. No one wishes to wade through forests of paper to find the vital points that have been decided at the meeting. In particular, minutes which regurgitate verbatim almost every comment of every individual present are guaranteed to produce maximum frustration in the reader.

So, here are some practical suggestions for producing minutes:

- Drafting minutes is a skilled function. *Identify an experienced minute taker* or train one up to do this job for you properly on a regular basis. Too often, the role of minute taker is seen as that of a dogsbody and is allocated on a rota basis among regular participants. Do you wonder that many sets of minutes are impossible to understand?

- Aim for *one side of A4 only*. Minutes should be an executive summary of what went on at the meeting. As such, they should contain the following:

  - the title of the agenda item
  - what was decided or action points
  - who is responsible for the next steps
  - the date for report back on progress

- *Add any further necessary information as appendices*. Sometimes it is important to publicize arguments for and against a certain course of action or note particular views, e.g. of a dissenting minority who wish their disagreement to be known. Don't, however, clog up the executive summary with this material. Rather, produce and attach an appendix containing the additional information as a separate document. Then make a note in the action column referring to the attachment so that those who wish to read it can do so and those who do not can move on rapidly unhindered.

Here is an example of a minutes sheet:

MEETING OF THE [MARKETING] DEPARTMENT				
Date: Tuesday 31 Jan 06		Time: 2.00pm	Duration: 2 hours	
Location: Room G5 – Landfill site				
MINUTES				
Item no	Item	Agreed that… (supporting information)	Action by	Report back date
1.	XYZ	123	Jo Bloggs	30 March
2.	ABC	456 (see Appendix A)	Fred Smith	25 February
3.	FGH	789	Jane Green	10 March
4.	KLM	234 (see Appendix B).	Sue Brown	30 April
5.	PQR	567	Jim White	

- Organize the *final version and distribution* of the minutes as soon as possible after the meeting. Participants need written back up of their follow-up action points.

Once all these practical issues have been sorted out, you will find your meetings take place only when necessary, and they will also be more organizationally efficient.

5.5 Quite apart from organizing meetings, I now have to chair them. What approach should I take to coordinating and managing the discussion so as to ensure an effective outcome alongside efficient management?

Excellent meetings chairmanship is a critical skill for people managers. It combines a number of other important skills, of which leadership and communication are but two. If you are able to run a meeting well, you will gain respect and trust, and will find that your own views very often carry the day.

Here are some **key issues** to take on board:

- If you are chairing, it is your meeting, therefore *plan meticulously* ahead of the event. It is unlikely that other participants will do so to the same extent (unless there is a serious political axe to grind) because they have other more pressing responsibilities. Go through the agenda, marshal your thoughts and views on each item, consider contrary views and arguments and have responses ready to counter them. In this way, your ability to persuade, coupled with your situational power, is likely to ensure that things go your way when the issue is one on which you have strong views

- *Seating positions* may be important. If there is an awkward matter to discuss where opposing views are strongly held, make sure that you have your closest supporter (preferably with some credibility of their own) sitting next to you. The chair's view put forward by a 'right hand man' is a powerful weapon in the persuasive armoury

- Call the meeting to order and begin with a brief 'welcome' statement and overview of the main matters for discussion and decision. This will set the tone and give participants a feel for how you are going to manage things. It therefore important from the outset for you to appear *assertive and confident*. You have the opportunity in this semi-formal environment to manifest your leadership skills to best advantage

- *Manage the various discussions*. Overall, it is important to structure the discussion so that views are presented in a systematic way. The presentation of opinions in a scattergun manner helps no one's understanding. So, take one set of views first, followed by any others. It is also a good idea to let participants have their say first before you express your own views. Make sure nobody hogs the limelight. Firmly thank contributors and invite someone else to speak if particular people go on for too long or start to repeat themselves. Ensure that 'wallflowers' are encouraged to have their say – don't ignore them, but rather supportively draw then into the discussion.
- *Watch the clock*. As time begins to run out, draw the discussion to a close, summarize the views expressed and agree next steps whether by general consensus or, if appropriate, by a show of hands.
- At the end of the meeting, *thank everyone* for their time in attending and their contribution, fix any date for a further meeting and finish on time. Don't be sidetracked by unimportant AOB!

In summary:

The ten golden rules for meetings

1. hold meetings only when necessary
2. have clearly defined objectives and outcomes
3. invite the right people
4. create an agenda
5. set timings
6. identify an appropriate location

7. plan meticulously
8. chair confidently
9. everyone to contribute
10. keep minutes brief

Summary

Here is a summary of some practical tips and techniques to help you deal with personal organization issues:

- Plan everything, but retain flexibility to allow for inevitable change.
- Organize your to-do list by prioritizing urgent and important tasks. Use your prime time when you are at your most effective for getting the critical things done
- Choose a diary system which works for you and use it for both appointments and blocked time for tasks.
- Deal with interruptions that get in the way of efficiency. Manage your approach to unscheduled people, emails, the telephone, paper clutter and your own tendency to procrastinate on difficult tasks.
- Set up meetings only when necessary. Ensure that timings, location, agenda, documentation and the right people are all organized or in place. Appoint a competent minute taker.
- Develop great chairing skills. Manage input wisely, keep thing moving, watch the clock, summarize and take a decision regarding next steps.
- Use the 10 Golden Rules of meetings to extract maximum output from them.

SIX
Delegation and coaching

6.1 As a people manager, I recognize that one of the key skills I should develop is the ability to effectively delegate tasks to my team. Why do I find delegating so difficult and scary?

Case study

Simon is a recently appointed team manager of a pharmaceutical research team. Last week for the first time he delegated a piece of chemical testing and analysis to a team member who made a complete mess of the assignment. This bad experience has immediately sapped Simon's confidence in his managerial competence. He feels that he cannot now trust people to get things right. He might as well do the job himself properly first time and thus error free. He is now frightened of losing control when delegating, but recognizes that he must delegate to maximize team output. On the other hand, he feels that if he delegates too much, he will become surplus to the company's needs? How can Simon overcome these anxieties?

You are right that delegation is an essential managerial activity and it is vital that you develop the skills required to do it well at the earliest opportunity. Delegation is, after all, the people manager's key organizational and time management tool.

Your anxieties about delegating are real, but there are rational responses to your fears which should help you to gain greater understanding of the need to delegate. Here are some of the more common problematic issues that managers raise:

- *'I've had a bad experience of delegating in the past, so it's not for me.'* One bad experience does not make the exercise a permanent nightmare. Learn from the problems of the past and develop the requisite skills to do things better and you will be amazed at how capable you become. In particular, get used to shouldering the responsibility that delegation entails. This is a key element in the process of your maturing as a manager.

- *'I don't feel confident enough to delegate.'* This lack of confidence stems either from fear of dealing with your people or fear of getting the process wrong. In the former case, you must develop your interpersonal and communication skills. This particular fear is one which will seriously impede your progress in the role of people manager if not addressed quickly. In the latter situation, again learn the practical process and skills of delegation, and confidence will grow with your increasing expertise.

- *'When I delegate, I experience major anxiety through loss of control over the delegated task.'* Yes and no. In delegating, you indeed do pass on a task to someone else to carry out, and you must trust them to get on with it effectively. However, part of the delegation process is to set up a monitoring system to check on task progress, and by doing this you will keep in touch with what is happening.

- *'I'm frightened of becoming redundant if, through delegating, my team is seen to be able to do everything without me.'* This shows that you have not yet understood your position as a people manager. You have a different job from the other members of your team, but it is all of you together who generate success. Without your coordinating leadership role, you can be sure that things would fall apart.

- *'I have no confidence in my team's capability to do delegated tasks.'* If this is true, you may have failed on two counts. First, you may not have recruited the right people or, in the case of an inherited team, made the personnel changes which you have deemed necessary. Second, you have not spent enough time on training and coaching team members to become competent in the work which you delegate to them. Recruiting and coaching are two of your key tasks as a people manager and you must allocate sufficient of your time to both of them.
- *'There are some tasks which I do perfectly myself. Why should I delegate them?'* Once you have reached this point with a task, then it definitively is time to delegate it, and for three reasons. First, you will now be doing the task instinctively and it is in this situation, interestingly, that you will start to make errors. Second, the task will no longer challenge you and it will have become boring to do. Third, to create a fresh development challenge for yourself, free up your time by delegating the task to provide a new challenge for one of your team members.
- *'By the time I've trained my team member and corrected any errors, I might as well have done the task myself.'* Training is certainly a time commitment, but it is a part of your job description as a people manager. Thus in committing time to training, you are not only fulfilling your role but making a skills investment in the team for the future which will provide its own payback many times over. And yes, mistakes will be made initially – that's part of normal human learning behaviour – but your role as manager is to commit further managerial time to providing effective feedback and so ensure that the reason for the error is understood and does not occur again.

If any of the above issues ring a bell with you, understand that they are normal managerial reservations, but that for each of them there is a positive solution.

6.2 Delegation is said to be one of the key organizational tools for people managers. What are the benefits of delegation and why should I develop the skills to make me a better delegator?

Delegation is the passing on of a task to someone else to do whilst retaining the overall responsibility for the success of that task. So you delegate the task itself together with whatever authority the team member needs to get the work done, but you as manager 'carry the can' and are accountable upwards if things go wrong (or bask in glory if the task is a resounding success).

Effective delegation benefits everyone – the organization you work for, your team member to whom you delegate a task and yourself. In a nutshell, the organization gains from an efficient use of its people resources; your team member gains by learning new tasks and related skills; and you gain by developing your managerial and leadership skills.

Here are some more specific **key benefits of delegation** which justify your developing excellent delegation skills:

- *It releases time for you to undertake your managerial role.* Remember that you are no longer a full-time technician. You will by now have delegated much of this technical element of your team's work. You have thus released time for yourself to think, plan and coordinate at a much more strategic level for your team and are able to focus on the leadership role for which you are now employed.

- *By delegating, you are developing your people management skills.* Quite apart from any formal training or coaching you may receive, every time you delegate, you are learning 'at the coal face' what works and what does not work for you in handling the process of delegation. You will make mistakes but will learn from them, developing particularly the skills you need to build working relationships with your team members.

- *Your team members learn and develop*. By undertaking delegated tasks, your team members acquire knowledge, skills and expertise which not only add significant value to the totality of the work effort, but assist them in developing their own work capabilities and thinking through potential career opportunities.
- *Delegation makes it more likely that you will achieve your team objectives*. When tasks are effectively delegated across the team in order to complete successfully, say, a project you are running, you are much more likely to hit your targets if team members know exactly what needs to be done, within what timescale and with what resources. In other words, your organizational skills, including delegation skills, have significantly contributed to the project's success.
- *Delegation is supportive of teamwork*. As team manager, you will explain to your team members, both as a group and individually, what needs to be done and by whom. By delegating in this way, team members understand that each of them plays a part in producing the end result of what the team is seeking to achieve. This underpins and supports teamwork.
- *Delegation encourages the development of a sense of responsibility*. When you delegate to a team member, he/she is empowered to carry out the task delegated. The team member is given authority to do what is necessary for the successful completion of the task and is accountable to you for its success. This accountability plus the delegated power, which helps ensure that something gets done, breeds a sense of responsibility both within the team member who takes pride in success, and towards you, stemming from the knowledge that you are responsible for the team's achievement in its relationship with the outside world. The development of a sense of responsibility is critical for career development.
- *Effective delegation results in an overall increase in business capacity*. If you delegate the right jobs to the right people at

the right time, this organizational efficiency means that you have created a working environment that ensures maximum productivity. The knock on effect for the business as a whole is huge in terms of output, cost savings and profitability. It is therefore vital for the business as a whole that your delegation skills are well honed.

From these examples, it is clear that delegation is an essential people management tool, the effective use of which will benefit all aspects of the business you work in.

6.3 I'm convinced that delegation is a critical activity and skills set which I need to develop, but how do I know what to delegate and who to delegate it to?

Let's deal with the '**what**' first. How do you decide which tasks to delegate and which to keep for yourself? Here are some general principles which might help your analysis. The starting point is to look at your to-do list, and decide which tasks are **procedural** only, i.e. in order to execute them little creative brain power is needed, and all that is required is the following of some simple instructions. Such tasks may well come from your unimportant task categories.

Examples might be: opening mail, reconciling sets of figures or filling in forms.

Procedural tasks so defined *must always be delegated*. You are too expensive/valuable to your organization to be spending time doing these basic non value-added tasks.

For all other tasks, you have a **discretion** as to whether to delegate or retain. These will be tasks that do require significant skill or expertise to carry them out, such as dealing with clients, making decisions, setting objectives or creating procedures. Subject to particular people skills (see below), there are four basic criteria which will assist you in making your delegation decision. Ask yourself this question: If you delegate, will the task be done:

- *Quicker* (faster as a result of greater dexterity, e.g. a trained typist word processing a long document when you would use a couple of fingers) and/or
- *Sooner* (completing the task earlier, e.g. this project will finish close of play Thursday if I delegate; if I do not, close of play Friday) and/or
- *Better* (one of my team has a superior skill to me for carrying out this particular task) and/or
- *Cheaper* (the cost to the organization will be less if I delegate this task)?

If you answer 'yes' to one or more of these criteria, and on balance, the yes's outweigh the no's, then delegate; otherwise retain.

This rule of thumb must be used with some caution. There may well be other factors which will influence your decision one way or another. In particular, your organization's culture or procedures may well prevent you delegating in some circumstances, e.g. because of specific rules relating to confidentiality or customer care. Subject to whatever constraints you are under, try to delegate as many tasks as possible.

Examples

Task examples – to delegate or not to delegate:

- Drafting a letter to a customer who has complained about poor service – DELEGATE: you have the opportunity to review the letter before it goes out.
- Checking and signing off your team's monthly report to the Board – DON'T DELEGATE: this is your last chance responsibility as team manager – but do delegate the production of the report itself.

- Sorting mail into urgent, non-urgent and junk. DELEGATE: this is a very basic procedural task, but train to ensure the terms urgent and non-urgent are properly understood.
- Giving an internal presentation on new working procedures which the team has set up. DELEGATE: this will be a great motivational exercise for them. Spread the work so as to avoid favouritism, and be there to provide support.
- Visiting a client who has just closed a substantial account. DON'T DELEGATE: the buck stops with you and this is a serious managerial issue which you should take care of.
- Checking the efficiency of the team's photocopying procedures. DELEGATE: another basic procedural task, but brief well beforehand (see 6.4 below).

One final word of warning here. Never delegate a task simply for the reason that you do not like doing it yourself. You will be resented if you do this. Make sure that the criteria are fulfilled first. If they are not, you keep the task and just put up with it.

The second issue is to **whom** we shall delegate. This should be a relatively straightforward decision. You have built your team using the guidelines discussed earlier and it should be clear who is the most appropriate team member to delegate to within the parameters of technical skills, generic skills and personality. In this context, it is worth revisiting and using the team building model discussed earlier.

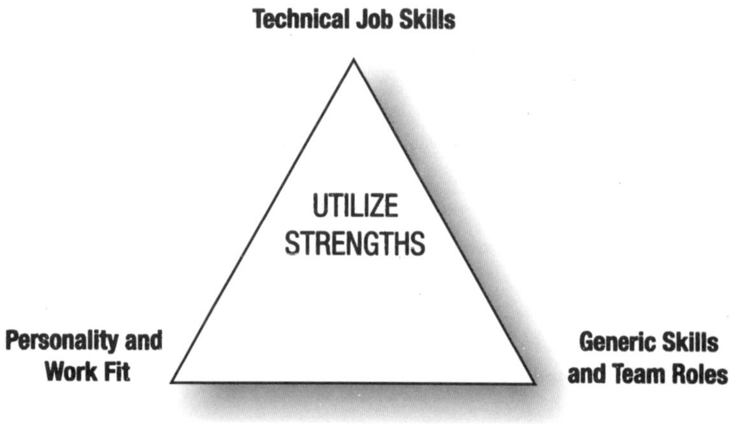

The Balanced Team

However, you may wish to delegate a particular task as a training exercise precisely to develop skills which the team member does not have at present. This is a good idea, but in this case the monitoring element of the delegation process will be critical (see below).

Here are two practices you should definitely avoid:

1. Giving the task to the first team member who is available. There is a tendency to do this particularly when you are under pressure. Take a deep breath and make a rational rather than an impulsive decision

2. Overloading a reliable team member who will always do the job well but eventually will be crushed by his/her workload. This practice is also unfair in team terms, letting off the hook those who are good at saying 'no', even unjustifiably, and to whom you may feel unable to face up

Do think through carefully this issue of 'who'. Get it wrong and you could be wasting much time and money.

6.4 The main problem I have with delegation is getting the process right so that both the people and task management issues are all successfully handled and I use my managerial skills to best advantage. What procedure should I adopt to ensure that what I delegate is well done?

The successful completion of a delegated task depends almost entirely on how well you handle the process of delegation. There is a series of well defined steps you should follow in order to achieve this.

1. Deal with the **'what' and 'who'** issues. The key considerations here were looked at in response to the previous question.

2. **Brief** the team member to whom the task is to be delegated. It is impossible to stress too highly the importance of this part of the process. You will need to set aside significant managerial time if the briefing is to be done effectively. As a guide to what you should be discussing at the briefing session, the mnemonic BOGSAT might be helpful. This is what it stands for and what each element should comprise:

    - *B = Background.* For motivational purposes, it is important that the team member understands the bigger picture into which his work fits. Tell him about the project as whole, why it is happening and, more broadly, how it will add value to what the organization is seeking to achieve. By doing this, the team member will feel involved and good about his contribution to team success.

    - *O = Objectives.* Set out the reasons why the task needs to be done. Explain the nature of the project in some detail and what the end result will be. Make sure that the team member has the key objectives in sight and is happy with why he has a part to play in delivering overall success.

- *G = Generalities*. This relates to the key elements of the task itself. Give the team member an overview of what he is to do. Outline the basic facets of the job so that once again he has a 'big picture' but this time of his own responsibilities.
- *S = Specifics*. Now get down to the detail of what needs to be done. Talk about resources, methodologies, sources of assistance, location, outcomes, expectations and anything else which will help the team member in achieving success with his task.
- *A = Administration*. These are details extraneous to the task but which will support the team member whilst the work is in progress. It may include paperwork responsibilities, e.g. completing progress sheets, or ensuring that any office equipment is available when it is needed. Most importantly, you should discuss at this stage how the delegated work will be monitored. Set up a system which is easy to remember and which includes face to face meetings.
- *T = Timings*. The team member needs to be aware of any timeframes within which he must work. This will include the deadline for completion of the task and, if the task is more complex, intermediate milestones along the way. Always try to bring the task completion date forward from its real deadline to allow for some slippage.

By remembering BOGSAT, it is unlikely that you will forget any of the critical matters of which the team member should be aware. In any event, ensure that you and the team member both ask copious questions throughout the briefing session, as well as at its conclusion, to ensure that everything has been understood.

3. Identify required **performance standards** and your consequent management style. This element of the discussion with the team member is concerned with how well you want the job done. It goes without saying that, as human beings, we will occasionally make mistakes at whatever skill level we are working. When this happens, good feedback should ensure that the mistake does not occur again. You only make any particular mistake once. But apart from this, you may need the delegated task done quickly and effectively by an expert with the potential error margin at or as near to zero as possible. Alternatively, you may give the job to a greenhorn as a practice exercise and learning run, when mistakes will be an integral part of the learning process. It is possible in fact to identify four levels of skill expertise in your team members:

   - *Beginner.* You will choose a beginner when the team member has no experience of the task in hand, there is no time pressure and mistakes are unimportant, i.e. this is to be a pure learning experience. Your management style here will be directive with heavy supervisory input and plenty of intervention.
   - *Learner.* Here the team member has some experience of the task, but is still not completely up to speed. Some mistakes may still occur. Here your style will be that of coach, providing plenty of encouragement, intervening where necessary and supporting the effort being made.
   - *Regular.* A regular is experienced in the task whilst still not an expert, is likely to make only the odd mistake and is normally able to spot problems before they arise. The most appropriate management style here is that of consultant, where you provide active advisory support, usually when the team member calls upon you to assist when they spot a potential problem.

- *Performer*. This team member is a reliable, skilled expert who will be given the task when time and accuracy are critical and is very unlikely to make any errors. Manage the performer by remaining 'hands-off', allowing them to run the show and simply keeping you up to date with progress. All you are required to do is coordinate the end result alongside other aspects of the project.

This analysis of team member competence and how you handle it can be aligned to the 4S leadership styles model discussed earlier. Using the terminology above, the matrix now looks like this in summing up performance standard/ style needs.

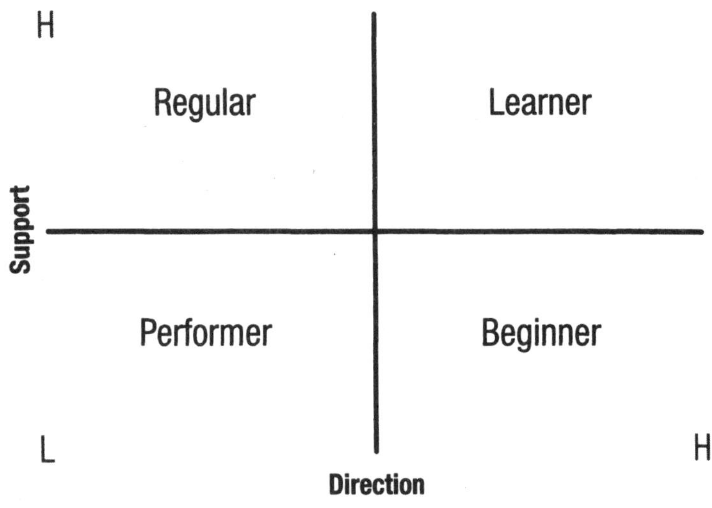

Delegation Performance Matrix

In terms of performance standards, therefore, choose the team member who best fits the circumstances surrounding the need to get the task done.

4. Organize any necessary **training or coaching**. It may be that before you require your team member to tackle the task, you want them to attend some formal training or undergo hands-on coaching from another more skilled team member. This may be particularly true for beginners and learners. If so, set something up which will directly help them develop their skills more quickly.

5. The team member **carries out the task**. Depending on what level of performance you are expecting, try to give some breathing space, even to beginners or learners. Most people like the challenge of attempting something themselves with minimum interference. Subject to appropriate management input, let them get on with it.

6. Since you have the responsibility for the ultimate success of the task, some form of **monitoring** progress both for your benefit and as a means of support for the team member is important. The level and frequency of monitoring will depend on whether you team member is a beginner, learner, regular or performer. Whatever monitoring procedure you think appropriate, make sure you discuss and agree the approach at the briefing session so that you team member is clear when and how the monitoring will happen. Ideally, fix a regular time for progress reports, but retain some flexibility on your availability to deal with other more urgent issues.

7. After briefing, the second most important activity forming part of the delegation process is giving the team member **feedback** on his performance. Giving feedback is something we all too often brush under the carpet. The task is finished, we are under pressure to move on to the next job and our thoughts focus on what's coming up. In reality, giving feedback is a critical part of the learning process for a team member and an essential element in developing the skills that turn a beginner into a performer. You must allocate management time to this activity. Feedback may be no more than a formal word of

thanks to a performer; for a beginner, the conversation may need significant time input on what went well and where lessons still need to be learnt. See 4.5 above for a more detailed discussion of how to give effective feedback.

8. If the task is a common one where you wish to move your beginner quickly down the track towards performer status, **repeat** this whole process on every occasion the task is carried out and observe how the team member's skills improve each time. Even if tasks are 'one-offs', always follow this delegation procedure to ensure that all the jobs you hand on are done effectively and efficiently, and that this is the result of using your own well developed management skills.

6.5 As a high performer in my previous technical role, I feel that I can make a major contribution in coaching my more junior team members towards improving their own technical skills. What does coaching involve and how should I go about it?

The first thing to understand is that coaching is not training. As an expert in your field, you can coach, but the nature of the coaching process means that non-experts can effectively coach as well. Thus as a people manager, even without your technical background, you will be able to make a significant coaching contribution to the development of your team's skills.

So **what is coaching**? It is process by which one person learns alongside another to:

1. unlock their natural ability
2. learn and achieve greater levels of performance
3. increase self-awareness of the factors which determine performance excellence
4. remove barriers to success.

The end result of successful coaching is that the team member will have moved through the four stage process of competence learning:

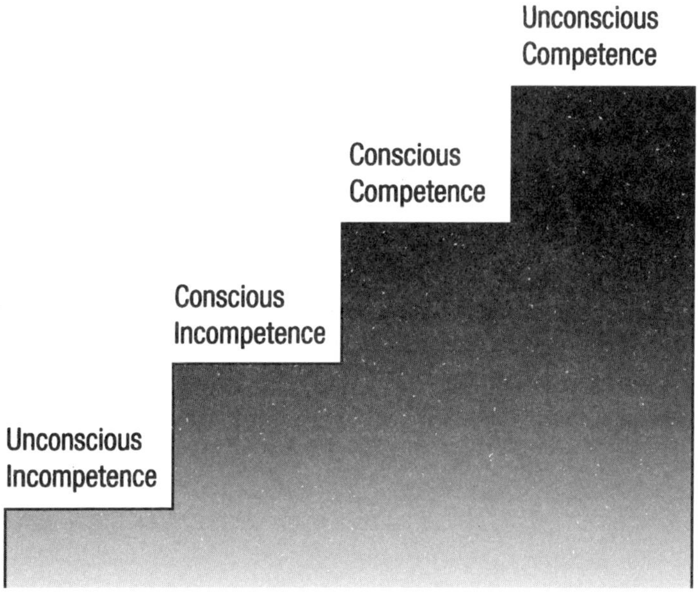

The Competency Staircase

So, coaching is a style and method of improving working practices and developing skills. A coach facilitates better performance in the person being coached. It is a generic skill and can be used in a number of work situations. In particular, there has been a marked recent increase in the use of external human resource consultants to improve the performance of senior executives. However, the classic uses of coaching for a people manager is in improving skills that are required to execute effectively either a delegated task or more generally to assist with career development. Coaching is in fact akin to what is known as 'action learning' – developing skills and understanding by actually doing the job itself – which many argue is the best way to learn work based competencies. The diagram below shows how much more receptive the human brain is to learning by doing.

	Told	Told and shown	Told, shown and experienced
Recall after 3 weeks	70%	72%	85%
Recall after 3 months	10%	32%	65%

Retention and Recall

The **skills** you need to be a good coach are first class interpersonal skills, including an ability to communicate effectively. As a coach, aim to develop the following attributes:

- *support* – do not take control but 'educate' in the literal sense of the word
- *interest* – be keen about what the team member is seeking to achieve
- *encouragement* – even when things go wrong
- *empathy* – develop rapport to create an element of teamwork in the venture
- *openness* – be prepared always to share ideas and say what you think
- *responsiveness* – be available to answer questions and advise when needed
- *trust* – develop an understanding so that the coaching relationship can flourish

If you aim to utilize a full complement of these skills, you will become an excellent coach.

The next issue is how to **structure** a coaching programme. What approach would you take to a coaching project which you wished to get involved in? Here is a useful mnemonic which will help you remember how to build a solid coaching process, namely, you need to STEER your team member in the right direction. So:

- S = *Spot* the coaching opportunity. Be alive to the various developmental activities which present themselves at work and suggest to the team member that coaching might be of help in a particular situation.

- T = *Tailor* the coaching to suit the need and the individual. Find out what approach will work best and agree a way forward and a coaching plan.

- E = *Explain* what needs to be done and how it might be done to improve performance, remembering to involve the team member in an 'educational' process.

- E = *Encourage* the team member to achieve the coaching target you have agreed by providing active support throughout the coaching period.

- R = *Review* progress as time goes on and when the coaching project comes to an end so that the team member can understand what has been achieved and what still needs to be worked at.

In effect the process involves, using the delegation terminology, you guiding your team member from a beginner to a performer, and this works particularly well when it is a technical skill that you are developing. The linkage between delegation and coaching in this context is instructive and as a process looks like the diagram overleaf.

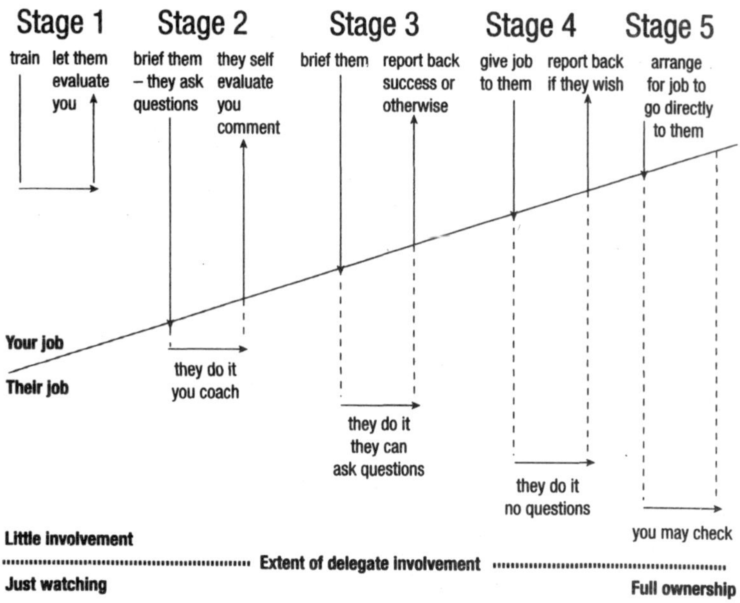

The Coaching and Delegation Process

The end result of coaching is that everyone **benefits** – your organization (by adding value to the business through the use of the skills developed and assisting with the succession planning process), you (by developing a stronger relationship with the team member and building trust for delegating tasks) and the team member (by building self-confidence, adding to his skills base and career development profile). So always be on the lookout for suitable opportunities to coach.

One final point. Remember that *coaching is not the same as mentoring*. A mentor is much more of a counsellor, helping to solve more general work problems, remove organizational barriers and give general career advice. Most importantly, a line or project manager cannot be a mentor to a member of his team. A mentor must be an independent colleague (or outsider) who is able to work with his charge without fear of favour.

6.6 As part of my training and coaching responsibilities, I need to understand how my team member is best able to learn and put into practice the new skills he is acquiring. Are there different ways of learning and differing approaches I should be taking with my team members as a result?

There are indeed different ways of ingesting new information and generally developing skills. The classic model which will help you understand how to approach a coaching assignment with a particular team member is Kolb's (later refined by Honey & Mumford) so called **Learning Cycle**. The model identifies four stages through which learners pass on their way to absorbing new skills. The model with its four stages is set out below:

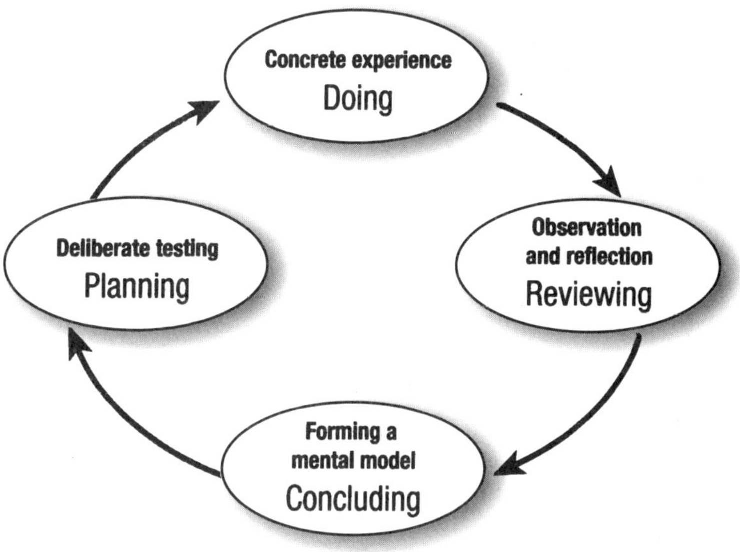

The Learning Cycle

We all have a preference for one or two of the stages as being those in which we feel most comfortable and from which we make the most progress in our understanding and competence. Nevertheless, we must pass through all the stages in the clockwise order set out in the model if we are truly to develop the skill we are seeking to acquire. Indeed, the cycle may well need to be gone through several times before any particular skill is fully mastered. The only issue is at which stage each of us should commence the learning process. We all have a preferred learning style. For adults, learning has to be relevant, proven, interesting and absorbable. These requirements are all satisfied when you as coach understand the starting point on the **learning cycle** from which your team member will maximize his learning experience. You start at that point, even if your own starting point is completely different. Failed coaching relationships often result from the coach making an assumption that the team member learns in exactly the same way as he does – which may not be true. Here are the learning styles based on the learning cycle.

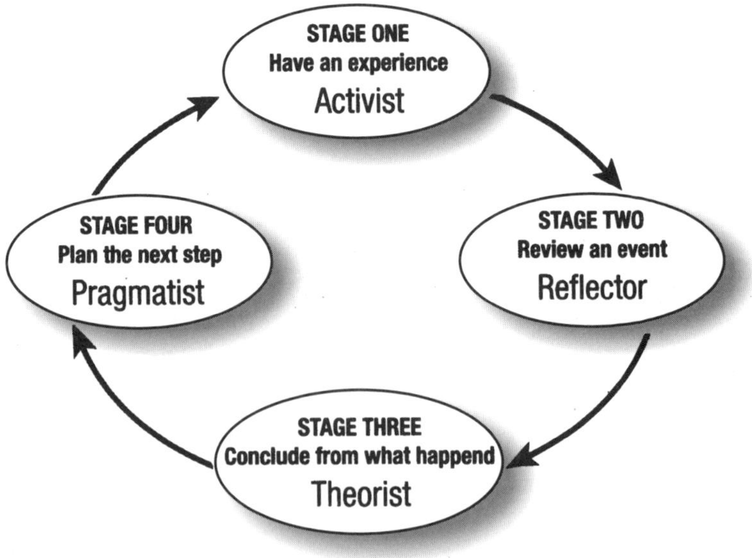

Learning Styles

A classic example is where an activist works with a theorist. The former needs to dive in the deep end, get his hand dirty, probably fail, but at least have acquired some practical experience up front. The theorist, on the other hand, will need to read the book of words first to gain a conceptual understanding of what the task is all about and only then will he think about actually doing something concrete.

Here is a synopsis of the key attributes of each learning style. When you notice a team member responding positively to a learning situation in one of these ways, that one will be his strongest learning preference.

- *Activists* get involved from the start. They enjoy immediate experiences and are open minded. Their motto is: 'I'll try anything once.' They act first and solve problems later through brainstorming. They thrive on challenges and get easily bored. They tend to be people centred and gregarious.
- *Reflectors* like to stand back and observe objectively from a distance. They collect data, analyze it and tend to leave decisions regarding the next step until the last minute. They are cautious, thoughtful and tend to take a back seat, preferring to listen to words of experience which they put into the melting pot of their considerations as to how to proceed.
- *Theorists* create models from their observations. They take a logical step by step approach to producing principles which form the basis of how things will eventually happen. Their motto is: 'If it's logical, it's good.' They have an air of detachment about them and are dedicated to rational objectivity. Their aim is to maximize certainty.
- *Pragmatists* like experimenting with new ideas and applications to see if they work in practice. They like to get on with things and act swiftly and confidently on theories that excite them. They are practical, sometimes impatient people who enjoy solving problems which they see as challenges. Their motto is: 'If it works, it's good'.

A variety of diagnostics is available to help you assess preferred leaning styles. Test your team members and, from the results, learn how best to approach a coaching or other leaning assignment with them.

It is worth mentioning in this context a further factor which could help in ensuring a successful learning outcome. There is a now well respected interpersonal communication process used by businesses across the world called **Neuro Linguistic Programming** (NLP). The idea behind NLP is to use various tools and techniques to develop closer rapport and understanding between individuals and thus create more productive working relationships. One of the basic distinctions which NLP draws is between the different receptive senses we use to communicate and how this can assist with the communication process. Each of us has a preferred sense for both imparting and receiving information. The three key senses are *sight* (visual), *hearing* (auditory) and *touch* (kinaesthetic). If you can discover which of these is preferred by your team member, you can play to that strength when considering how to assist with the learning experience.

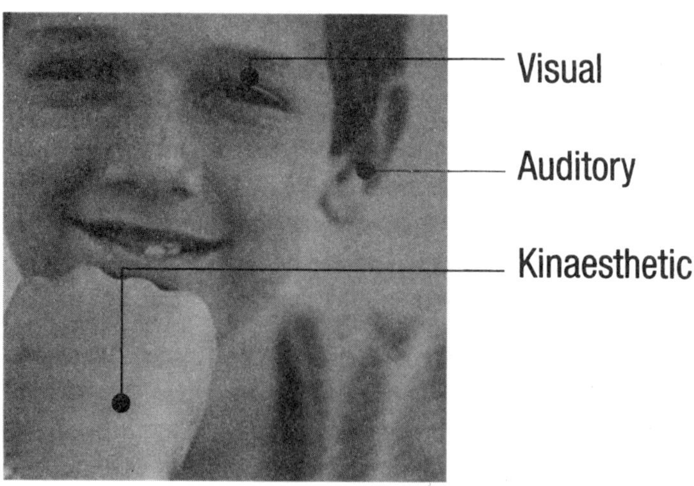

NLP Receptors

- So an *auditory* is a 'words' person and will respond well to oral explanations or information imparted via written text. An auditory excels through hearing.
- A *visual* is a 'pictures' person and likes diagrams, charts, graphs and other similar pictorial representations, or likes watching a demonstration. A visual excels through seeing.
- The *kinaesthetic* is a 'feeling' person who needs to get his hands on the job by picking up and using any piece of kit which is part of the learning process. Practical working with the hands is crucial to this type. A kinaesthetic excels through touching.

Find out, again by use of an appropriate diagnostic, which is your team member's preferred sense and lock in to that when explaining a coaching point.

Summary

Here is a summary of some practical tips and techniques to help you deal with delegation and coaching issues:

- Overcome the fears of handing over responsibilities to other people.
- Recognize that you must develop trust, and be prepared for imperfection, mistakes, extended time frames and the frustrations of not doing it perfectly yourself first time.
- See delegation as a managerial self-improvement exercise. Focus your mind on the real benefits of delegating to your organization, your team members and yourself.
- Be clear that a particular task is an appropriate one to delegate, and select the right team member to do it using the team skills triangle.
- Create a process for how to delegate effectively. In particular, make sure you brief your delegate comprehensively and do not

omit to spend time giving him feedback when the task has been completed.

- Develop skills to coach team members – show support, interest and encouragement, and use a structured procedure such as the STEER model to help you achieve your coaching ends.
- Be sensitive to the learning styles of your team. Get to know which style works best with individual members and accelerate the learning process by adopting it. Consider whether the NLP classification will add value to the process.

SEVEN
Stakeholders

7.1 As a people manager, I am not solely concerned with the members of my own team but need to build relationships outside the team to ensure that we are generally recognized and supported both within our organization at large, and indeed outside it. How do I make sure that I am aware of everyone with whom I should be building these relationships?

What we are talking about here is building a *network of stakeholders* in your success, how you identify them and what sort of relationship you should be developing with each of them.

Who are my stakeholders?

A stakeholder is anyone who is affected by your team's activities and their outcomes. This definition spreads the net far and wide, and it would be worth your while to sit down once you have settled into your role and to list all those who fall into this category. You will be amazed at how many people can affect your team's performance.

As a starting point, include all those who fit within the following descriptions:

- *From whom do we need goods and services to enable us to undertake our tasks?* Here you will list internal and external suppliers. Given your team's function, include as many colleagues as are relevant from the following: purchasing, office services, HR, marketing, accounts, IT and external sources of all or any of the foregoing.

- *Who has to use or live with our output?* Into this category will fall your own team and its customers. Your customers may be internal (e.g. your team delivers IT support to the organization) or external (you provide professional services to paying clients).
- *Who can help us deliver our targets?* Arguably, this is the most critical of all the categories, for here you will include relevant senior management people and senior representatives of your customers, all of whom have positional power to make things happen on your behalf. Critically, your own direct line manager is included here.

Try using a mind map to help identify your stakeholders like this:

Then remember to add at the next level the *names of the specific individuals* with whom you need to develop the relationships, i.e. sort out the 'who?'.

Having done this, *make appointments* to visit the critical people on your list and at least speak to the others on the telephone. You need to introduce yourself and ensure people know who you are. These are your stakeholders outside the team. You will have undertaken this exercise already with your own team members.

7.2 Should I treat all stakeholders the same, or are there different approaches to be taken when dealing with each?

You must deal with different stakeholders in different ways, not only because you do not have time to spend hours constantly relating to each one, but the value added that each offers you will differ depending on their role and how important they are to your team's success. So, to differentiate between stakeholders, analyze their position using the technique known as stakeholder mapping.

Stakeholder mapping looks at two issues and plots them against each other into a classic four box matrix using high/low grading. These issues are 'support' and 'influence'. So you should ask yourself:

1. How much influence does this stakeholder potentially have in helping my team achieve their objectives?
2. How much direct support does my team get from this stakeholder?

The map then looks like this:

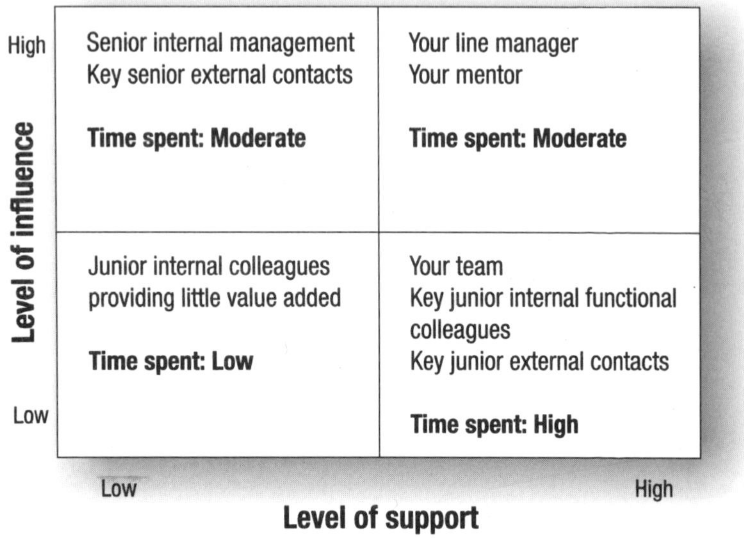

Stakeholder Map

So, think through who goes into which box and, as before, put real names against the role.

One point you may think controversial is why those with high influence are only allocated a moderate amount of your managerial time. The reason for this is that most of your working hours must be spent with those who are helping you to achieve objectives at the coal face. What the matrix does not show is that the moderate amount of time spent with high influencers must be top quality time, so that when you *are* devoting your attention to them, you are maximizing the value-added returns. These people do not like to be ignored.

7.3 Having identified and categorized my stakeholders, how and what should I be communicating with them to ensure maximum returns on my networking investment?

The stakeholder mapping matrix should also be used to determine the 'what' and the 'how' of stakeholder communication and they vary as follows:

- *Low influence/low support.* Here, minimal communication effort only is required. These people are low value stakeholders. Emails on general issues affecting them will do.
- *Low influence/high support.* These are your people who are delivering the team objectives on a day to day basis. Make sure they know everything that directly impacts on their jobs. You work very closely with them, so maximize your use of human contact communication as your preferred approach.
- *High influence/high support.* These are the key people – the more senior colleagues with a direct interest in your outcomes, in particular your boss. Give them not only everything they want but also everything you think they ought to know. This is an issue of judgement learnt over time. Remember in particular to cope with matters that are clearly within your delegated responsibility. Use all major forms of communicating here.
- *High influence/low support.* These are the senior people who are removed from you on a day to day basis but have power to intervene if necessary. Ask them directly what they would like to know about your department's work and pander to their wishes. A copy of the occasional milestone email or a phone call to ask for advice may be all that is needed.

The reworked matrix map below summarizes this approach to stakeholder communication.

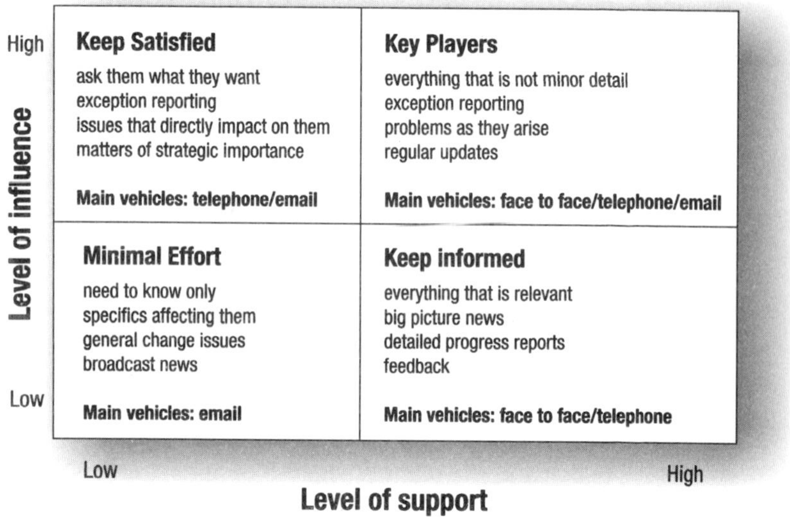

Stakeholder Communication

Case study

Q was a member of the HR team of a global financial services operation. He had specific responsibility for professional development and training in the corporate banking division. Q sat down with representatives from the banking team to discuss the introduction of e-learning as an at-the-desk option for juniors to get to grips with basic banking principles. Q and the banking team got hold of a selection of packages from a variety of providers, watched demos and eventually placed an order for the best package for the job. The CDs arrived, but it soon became clear that the bank's IT system did not have the right platform to support the software and a significant amount of money invested in the CDs was lost. Q had failed to identify a senior IT systems manager as a key stakeholder in the project and subsequently failed to either involve him or communicate with him about the suitability of the e-learning package.

Summary

Here is a summary of some practical tips and techniques to help you deal with stakeholder issues:

- Identify who are your stakeholders. Brainstorm a series of 'who' questions designed to bring everyone who assists you in getting the job done to the forefront of your mind. Use mind mapping techniques to help with this exercise.
- Visit or at least phone those outside your team to assist you in understanding the right sorts of relationship you need to develop.
- Undertake stakeholder mapping using the influence/support matrix to enable you to see the relative levels of importance of the people with whom you should relate.
- Create a communication strategy so that the right stakeholders receive the right messages and the right amount of your attention in the right way.

EIGHT
Communication skills

8.1 As a people manager, I need to develop working relationships with my team members. What is the starting point for achieving this?

If there is one word which sums up the foundation upon which all human relationships are built, it is 'communication'. Whether we are at home, at work or on holiday, all the relationships that we necessarily build in these environments more or less succeed depending upon how well we communicate with those we deal with.

At work, when you take over a new team, your first task is to get to know your direct colleagues. Many of them you may never have met before. How do you then go about starting the relationship ball rolling?

Imagine (because it is easier) that you have set up an inaugural drinks reception for the team and have been introduced to a colleague you have not met before. The development of the conversation (and potentially the relationship) may well go through the following stages:

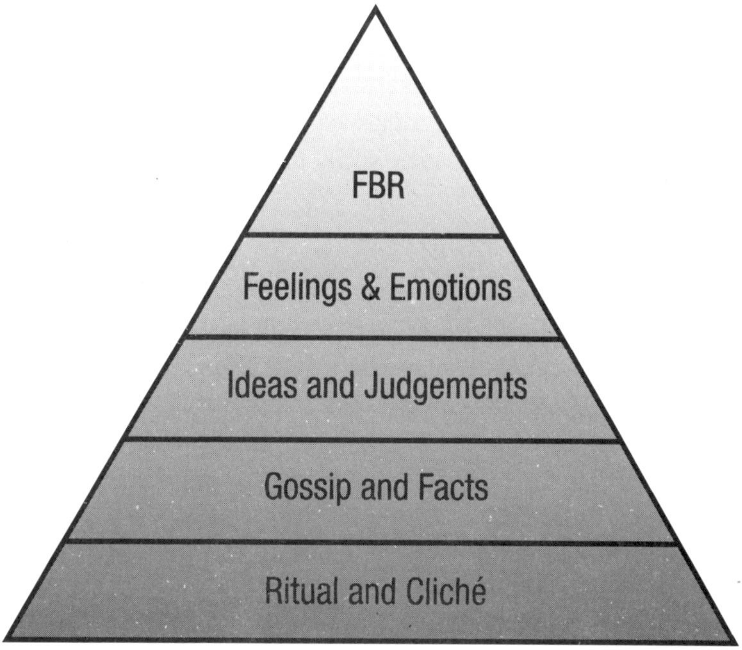

Levels of Communication

1. At the most basic level you may talk about the weather, how you arrived at the event, perhaps where you live, how good or bad a turnout it is and the quality of the refreshments. All this is harmless banter – or **ritual and cliché** – held at arms' length whilst you sum up the person before you. There is no real 'getting to know you' at this stage.

2. Assuming you don't move away at this point (and as that person's people manager, you cannot), the conversation will rise to level two as you begin to relax a little together. This is the **gossip** stage where you start to talk about people you know, how they enjoy working in the organization, discover what your favourite sport is or generally share facts which start to indicate whether or not you have things in common on which a fuller relationship can be based.

3. If stage two has been successful, you should be thinking that here is someone I may be 'able to do business with' and you will move on to level three which involves sharing **thoughts and ideas** on topics of mutual interest. These may be commercial issues, social matters, or even how your local football team can improve its performance. Unless you are willing for things possibly to grind to a halt at this point, avoid the usual politics and religion.

It is unlikely that things will progress much further at the reception, and, indeed, it is a sad fact of working life that very often this is the point at which relationship development ceases. The level three conversations of course progress to high level discussions about direct day to day working issues. But there is no additional movement towards 'feeling' how you and your team members can further develop your working relationship. Do therefore attempt to move the relationships over time (and it will take time) to:

4. Here you are sufficiently confident about each other to 'let your hair down' and be open and honest about feelings for and **emotional reactions** to particular work issues. By moving to this level of communication, you gain a much more rounded picture of each other which in turn instils greater understanding of what makes you tick, your likes and dislikes, and your potential reactions to change and other challenging work situations. So dig over time to discover what your team member *feels* about various significant issues. Armed with this information, you have a much better chance of making decisions and generally running the team in a way which is sensitive to the needs and reactions of its members.

5. FBR stands for **full-blown relationship**! You arrive at this stage when you have known and related to someone for so long that you almost live inside each other. This level of communication is manifested by finishing off the other person's sentence, or knowing what the person will say before

they say it. On a purely personal level, this is a cozy position to be in and one you will observe (or experience) with a spouse or long standing partner. In the work context, however, it is potentially *dangerous* to arrive at this depth of understanding, if only because you may get the 'vibes' of where the team member is coming from wrong. A business mistake resulting from instinct about another person's position may be extremely costly. Therefore avoid (or at least double check assumptions arising from) FBRs at work.

One final point here. Developing excellent communication skills has got nothing to do with liking somebody. We meet and work with many people in life – some we get on with very well, some we know we have difficulty with and the rest we are fairly neutral about. Statistically, this pattern follows a normal distribution curve and there is nothing we can do about that.

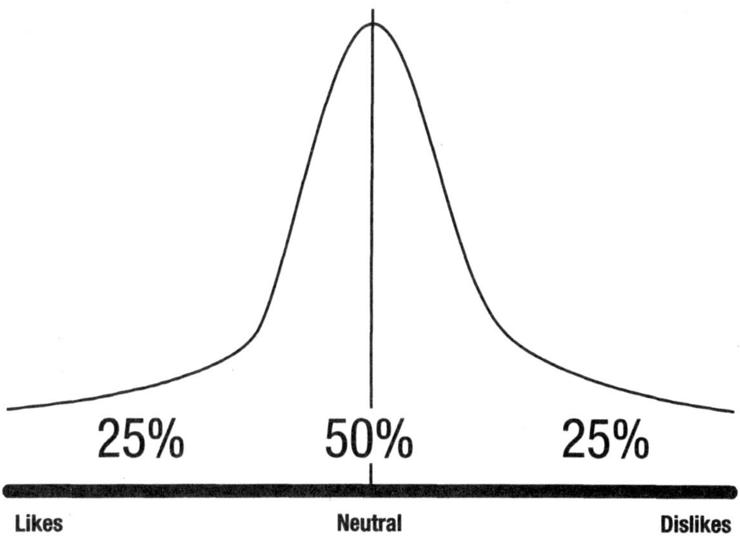

The Normal Distribution of Instinctive Relationships

If you acquire a new team, it is unlikely that you will get on famously with everyone. Differing personalities are a fact of life and you may have someone in the team who is an awkward character but extremely skilled at the job they do. With someone like this, it becomes all the more important to make the effort to reach level 4. It will be well worth it to gain greater understanding of that team member and improve communication accordingly.

In conclusion, what happens as you move from level one to level four is that you are closing the distance gap – wide when you meet someone for the first time and know nothing about them (stranger); narrow when you have got to know them well and are working with their feelings as well as their rational thoughts (close colleague).

8.2 There are now a wide variety of communication methodologies which I can use to communicate with my team. Are there any ground rules for determining which method I should use for getting across particular information?

Marshall Macluan, the US marketing guru of fifty years ago, coined the phrase 'the right medium for the right message'. Although his remark was directed at the consumer sales industry, the principle remains good for all communications strategies whatever their context. So, as a people manager you should remember that phrase when determining how to get your message across to your team or elsewhere.

The diversity of methodologies available to you is illustrated in the scattergram below which plots the complexity of the message against the emotional reaction it might generate.

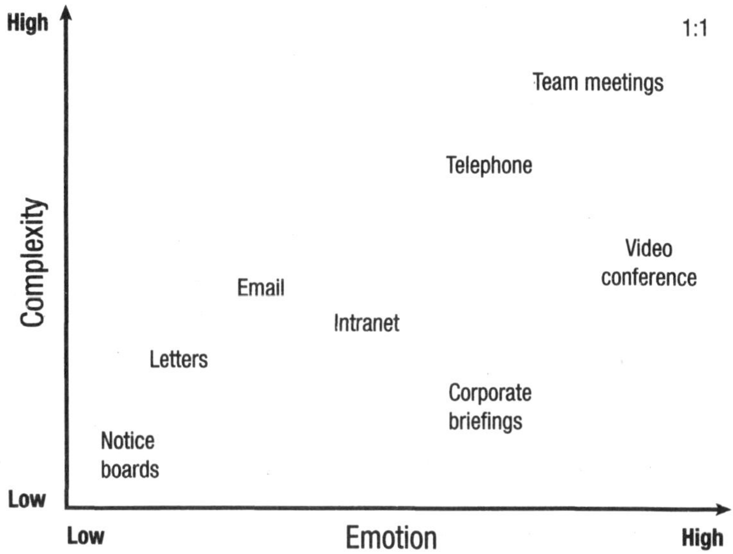

Communication Vehicles

What this shows is that, like the narrowing of the gap between people as they get to know each other, the communication methodology should reflect the distance that is appropriate for the particular message that you need to get across. The more personal and important the message, the more likely it is that you will need to employ a face to face conversation.

So here is a list of the key communication methodologies and some suggestions as to when each might best be used:

1. **IT networks**. Your intranet is an important internal marketing tool, but is highly depersonalized and the likelihood of everyone seeing all the information placed upon it is well below 100%. So use the intranet for non-urgent information which is also non-critical in day to day business terms. General policy statements, minutes of meetings, success stories and social events are ideal for this medium.

2. **Letters**. These are a classic 'distance' medium when used in the internal context and are now confined solely to formal employment issues – hiring, firing, resignation and changes to terms and conditions. Do not use them within your team in any other context.

3. **Fax and memos**. Both these methods of communication are now obsolescent, having been superseded by emails and email attachments. They can still be used as a fallback when IT systems go down, and the fax might be helpful if you are running a remote international team in a location where technology is still catching up with the First World. Both are personal but distant forms of communication. See emails below for when to use.

4. **Emails**. The email is the most used and the most misused form of communication in the 21st century. It is quick, cheap, readily available for outgoing use and readily accessible for incoming messages both at the work station and remotely. It can be used as a stand alone dispatcher of electronic memos, or be the vehicle for sending letters and more complex documents as attachments. Access to a printer ensures that hard copy is available if needed.

   But it remains an impersonal form of communication. Use emails (like faxes and memos) only for imparting information where the message is bland, relatively unimportant or uncontroversial, i.e. where there is no level four emotional input for either the sender or the recipient. For any communication where a reaction is likely, only use email as a confirmatory follow up to an initial telephone conversation or face to face discussion where the issues have been initially aired.

   Too often, email is misused, acting as an apparently safe haven for those unable to face up to personal contact through lack of self-confidence. There have been instances of colleagues emailing each other when they sit in close proximity in an open plan office. The most appalling example in recent years in the UK was the sacking of a large number of employees in a financial services organization by SMS texting (shorthand email)! *Email must never replace necessary human contact.* Some businesses have been so worried by this depersonalized trend in communicating that they have banned internal emails on Fridays. If you need to communicate in that environment, you have to telephone or walk to find colleagues. Try introducing this practice in your own business.

5. **Telephone and teleconferencing**. The telephone brings you a step nearer to full human contact. Here you have a voice to listen to, so it is possible to gauge reaction to what is being said through tone of voice as well as being able to converse immediately on the subject matter of the call. Use the telephone to discuss semi-important matters where it would be helpful to exchange views and ideas with the other party or parties, or where it would be discourteous or tactless not to hold some sort of conversation when imparting a particular piece of information.

6. **Meetings**. Meetings provide a real time opportunity for presenters to be seen as well as heard in a fully people-focused setting. They can take a number of forms, from the weekly team briefing, through road shows to a major internal corporate presentation. Use briefings/presentations when there is an important global message to impart which is likely to elicit some general reaction. The meeting then provides a forum for feedback, question and answer sessions and more general interaction to explain more fully some of the issues, answer queries and resolve anxieties.

7. **Video conferencing**. This requires a brief word in its own right. Video conferencing is a useful tool for holding meetings when participants are at a distance. The key to success here is to ensure that the technology is working effectively.

Time delays plus malfunctioning visual or audio equipment can readily destroy the otherwise advantageous nature of the session. There is nothing more disconcerting, for example, than to be participating in a video conference for several minutes before hearing a disembodied voice pipe up from outside camera shot!

8. **Face to face/one to one meetings**. These should be reserved for the more important communication events where individual issues are the subject matter of the discussion or confidentiality is vital. One to one meetings tend to be under valued. Be prepared to use them more frequently. They are essential for performance management meetings, individual feedback sessions and career progression discussions. Also use them when you need to tap in to the views of a trusted colleague who has the experience to help with you making a particular decision. Whatever the circumstances, remember that a one to one meeting is the closest individual communication vehicle available to you and is the most powerful medium for getting things done through others.

8.3 As a team leader, I wish to encourage my team members to understand and share my vision for what we should be doing and developing for the future. How do I set about achieving this?

Communication, we have suggested, is the ultimate road towards great working relationships. But why do we communicate in our working environment, particularly as a people manager with our team members? The answer is to **influence** why, what and how the team performs.

So, we communicate to influence. Effective *influencing is a skill,* and it is this critical people management skill which you must develop above all others in order to carry out your role to best advantage.

Whom must you influence? All those you have business dealing with – clearly your team, but also senior management, external advisors, consultants, customers, clients and anyone else you with whom you necessarily come into contact. In a nutshell, you need to influence all those who are stakeholders in the success of your role.

Why is influencing so important? Because it is only through influencing that you can effectively encourage people to go along with your ideas, views and ways of doing things. This has always been true when you are operating outside the team, but try telling a team member what to do in our current social and employment climate and you will get short shrift. Influencing is now a critical motivational tool within the team as well as outside it.

Case Study

An engineering company decided to install a new machine tool into its production line. It did this after much research, but it failed to consult the shop floor operatives who would be working the machine. The machine was in fact much less effective than it might have been had the operatives been involved in the specification process. Consequently, they were demotivated in having to use second rate equipment. Management realized that things were not as successful as they had hoped and at that stage consulted the shop floor. The resulting expert input influenced them to replace the new machine with a different model. This now did the job, productivity increased and the operatives were happy working with' their' machine tool.

How then do we become a great influencer? The answer lies in developing a skills sub-set which we can call 'The 7 Deadly Skills' – deadly, in the sense that if you become expert in using all of them appropriately, you become irresistible and the world falls on its knees in the face of such a successful communication onslaught!

Here are the **7 Deadly Skills** to develop:

1. ask great questions
2. listen attentively
3. use appropriate body language
4. develop assertiveness
5. use powerful persuasive techniques
6. maximize impact by presenting the right image
7. create a sense of rapport

For the purposes of discussing the 7 Deadly Skills, you should assume that you are holding a face to face conversation. Whilst some of the skills work well when using other communication vehicles, it is only during one to one personal interactions that all seven come together. Thus these skills are critical particularly as a means of developing excellent interpersonal relationships.

8.4 I understand that in order to obtain information, I must ask incisive questions. What types of question can I usefully ask, and are there any which I should avoid?

The aim behind asking questions is to obtain accurate information from the person with whom you are speaking. In this context, there are indeed types of question you can validly use and some that will simply confuse or generate inaccuracies. Here are some different types of question:

1. Valid questions

- *Open questions*. These are those which are designed to elicit maximum information from the person with whom you are speaking. They often begin with the word 'what', 'why', 'how' or 'when'. They are called 'open' because there is no limit imposed on the amount of information which may come back. To be accurate, the answer must be full and extensive – it is impossible to respond to 'how', for example, without going on at some length. Here are some examples of open questions which might be used when discussing a work issue with a team member:

- *What procedure did you follow when servicing that machine?*
- *Why has client X decided to take his business elsewhere?*
- *How did you manage to persuade Mr Y to join our team?*
- *When will we be able to see positive results from our marketing initiative?*

Notice that these questions are quite precise. Open questions should not be so open that they allow the respondent to waffle. 'Tell me about yourself' as an interview question is relatively useless, but 'Tell me about the role you filled with your last employer' is much more likely to yield useful information.

- *Probing questions*. These usually follow open questions, and may be seen as open questions in their own right, except that they are designed to pick up and expand on basic information gleaned from the initial open question. Here are some examples based on the open questions above:
  - *What difficulties did you encounter during the servicing?*
  - *How was it that we failed to pick up on client X's unhappiness?*
  - *Why was Mr Y pleased with our personal development programme?*
  - *How might we be able to bring forward the date of the launch of our brochure?*

  Probing questions can be asked in a series one after the other until you get to the nub of a particular problem. At this point you may wish to move onto.....

- *Closed questions.* These demand a straightforward either/or answer. Usually it is 'yes' or 'no', but could be 'black' or 'white' or any other similar clear cut alternatives. You will ask a closed question when you are seeking a very specific answer to determine a state of affairs, or to check on the accuracy of something that has been said earlier. Closed questions are said to be confirmatory in their nature, i.e. used at the end of a conversation as the final 'full stop', but it is also possible to commence a conversation with a closed question before moving on the open or probing ones, e.g. 'Did you go abroad for your summer holiday this year?' Whether this elicits a 'yes' or 'no' answer, you can follow it with an open question beginning with 'why?' or 'where?'.

- *Reflecting/summarizing questions.* Use these when you wish to check on understanding either at a crucial milestone in the conversation or at the end of it. It is particularly important to do this where you have been talking for some time and may have forgotten some point that has been agreed, or you want to check the accuracy of the notes you have been taking. An example of a summarizing question might be: 'So what we have agreed is........?'

- *Hypothetical questions.* These are helpful to assist the other side to understand a difficult point you are trying to make. We all occasionally experience the situation where we have a mental block when trying to understand an issue that someone is attempting to explain to us. When this occurs, think of an analogous situation (often a sporting example works well) and talk the other side through this first, e.g. 'Suppose that we were experiencing this [on the football field], how would things work out here?' When the person you are talking to grasps the answer to this parallel question, you can move back to the real scenario and usually find that things are now understood perfectly.

2. Invalid questions

A question is invalid if it is couched in such a way which it could lead to an inaccurate answer. Here are some examples:

- *Leading questions*. Lawyers understand these perfectly and use them when cross-examining witnesses. You should not, however, use them because you are not in the business of trying to induce, for example, your team member to say something which may not be true. Thus avoid asking questions such as:
  - *You will be able to work overtime this evening, won't you?*
  - *You did check the accuracy of those sales figures, didn't you?*
  - *You are qualified to use this machine, aren't you?*
- *Multiple questions*. Here you ask several questions rolled into one, or fire off a number sequentially without waiting for the answers to those that went before. Either way, this is designed to confuse. The answer(s) you get will not be comprehensive because not all questions have been remembered, or worse, the person answering will be selective, responding only to those questions to which he knows the answer. This last situation can work to the responder's advantage, e.g. in a panel recruitment interview when two or more panellists ask questions contemporaneously, allowing the interviewee the chance to pick the one he knows most about. So do not ask questions like this:
  - *How did you deal with that client? Why has he taken his business elsewhere? What went wrong with the job we were doing? What lessons have you learnt from this episode?*
- *Limiting questions*. These, by definition, are phrased in such a way as to restrict the amount of information coming back. For example: 'What were you doing driving on the M1 last

Friday?' precludes an answer which might suggest that the other side was on the M1 last Thursday or that last Friday he was on the M11. Clearly, by asking such questions, you may not get back all the information you need and thus see the full picture regarding the circumstances under discussion.

- *Assumption-laden questions.* This type of question is based on a supposed set of 'facts' or a conclusion drawn from facts which may not be true. Thus the question: 'Why are you going to an interview for a new job without talking to me first?' based on you seeing, unusually, your team member wearing a smart suit is based upon an assumption that suit = interview, when there may be a number of equally cogent explanations as why the suit was being worn that day.

8.5 I am told that I am not a very good listener and that this upsets and annoys those with whom I am conversing. How can I improve my listening skills?

Listening is arguably the most important of the 7 Deadly Skills. If you were to ask colleagues what gives them most confidence and comfort in you as a leader, and develops most their sense of trust in you, they would undoubtedly say 'he listens to our views' or 'he hears what we have to say'.

So what is listening and what must you do to become a good listener? The first thing to understand is that there are various activities we call listening, but which do not amount to the sort of listening we are seeking to develop as an influencing skill. There are in fact four different levels at which we use our ears:

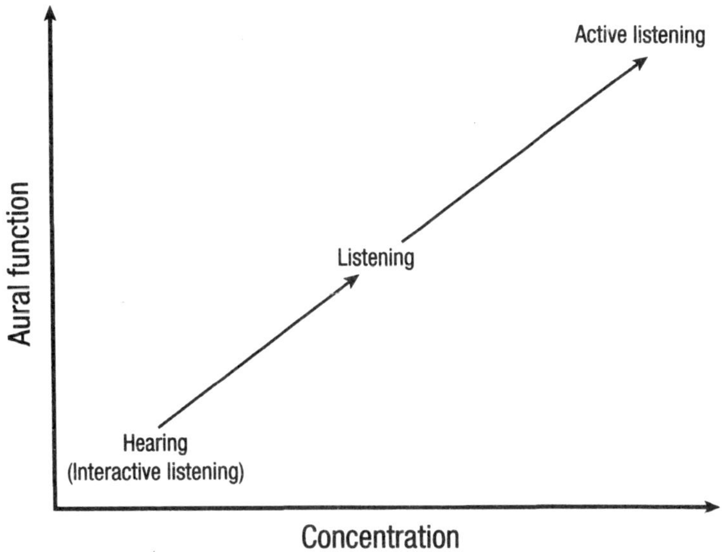

The Four Levels of Listening

- **Level 1 = Hearing**. Notice this is not listening; it is simply the subconscious use of our ears which acts, for example, as an early warning system if suddenly some unusual noise impacts on our brain. In our increasingly noisy world, sounds are imposed upon us all day long – office hubbub, traffic outside, photocopiers clanking, the whirr of air-conditioning etc – but we do not listen to these sounds. We simply hear them subconsciously, accept them as part of the environment and concentrate on everything else which we have to get done.

Example

Suppose you move to live close to a railway line. At first, you will find the noise of the trains consciously disturbing, possibly waking you up early in the morning. But soon you will accept these sounds as they drop away into you subconscious, only noticing them when guests remark on the noisy trains and how do you put up with them. Some time later, you take a short break in the countryside, and find you cannot sleep because there are no trains. You are disturbed by silence, a breeze in the trees or birdsong.

At work, level one hearing is clearly not an option when it comes to listening to your colleagues.

- **Level 2 = Simple Listening**. You will be surprised to learn that this is still not good enough. Simple listening does not include the right amount of concentration required to effectively absorb what is being said to you. Have you noticed those occasions in conversation when the person you are speaking to appears to be taking in what you are saying, but their eyes are telling you that their real thoughts are miles away? Have we not ourselves been guilty of this, concentrating on our input to the meeting taking place in an hour's time or itching to get away to a more interesting person on the other side of the room, rather than focusing on the person in front of us? We appear to be listening, but the reality is that our concentration is superficial.

Level 2 Listening does not reach the required skill standard you are seeking to achieve to become a great influencer.

- **Level 3 = Proactive Listening**. This is where our listening skills should be. Real listening requires energy and effort, and it is only through proactively focusing in this way that we produce the right amount of concentration needed to absorb the information coming across to us. Effective listening is hard work and tiring. Think about a situation where this sort of concentration is vital.

Example

Manager X has advertised to fill a middle ranking technical position in his department. He sifts the applications and calls six candidates to interview on a particular day, organizing things so that he will see three in the morning and three in the afternoon. Each interview will last 45 minutes followed by 15 minutes of reflection and writing up notes. X needs the right person for the job and knows that he must concentrate hard to ensure a successful appointment. At the end of that day, X is mentally exhausted and emotionally drained. And for most of the time he has done 'nothing' but listen.

As a people manager seeking to influence, you should develop your listening skills to level 3 proactive listening.

- **Level 4 – Interactive Listening**. This level is 'nice but naughty'. Notice from the graph that it virtually goes back to square one requiring little if any aural effort or concentration. You will know a number of people – your domestic partner, longstanding colleagues or friends – with whom you are so close that you know what they are going to say before they say it. In other words, you are hearing in this situation an unspoken statement, the essence of which is based on your instinctive understanding of what they will say. Nine times out of ten your hunch as to what would/will be said may be right, but there is always the possibility that you may be wrong. For this reason, interactive listening in a business context is *dangerous and should be avoided*. The problems associated with it correspond with the FBR level of communication. However well you know a colleague, always wait for the answer, listening to it proactively, before acting on what may be a potentially false assumption.

Here are some final **tips for great listening:**

- *Don't interrupt.* Allow the speaker to finish what he is saying before responding or commenting. Interrupting is rude.
- *Show occasional recognition* and understanding by a slight nod of the head, 'uh-huh', 'mmm' or 'I see'.
- *Watch out for body language* (see below) as a possible indicator of hidden messages – and be conscious of your own!
- *Take brief notes* – this is a great confidence booster to the other side that you are interested in what they have to say.
- *Avoid distractions* – make sure you are not subject to people and telephone interruptions.

8.6 What is body language and why is it so important that my body language is correct when holding a conversation? What in particular should I be aware of?

The reason body language is so important is that the credence given by the other side to what you are saying and how you yourself view the importance of the conversation is determined by a whole body experience as seen by the other side.

The impact of a face to face message is determined by three factors – what is said (which accounts for some 15% of the message), how it is said (30%) and, way ahead as the most important factor, the body language used by the speaker (55%).

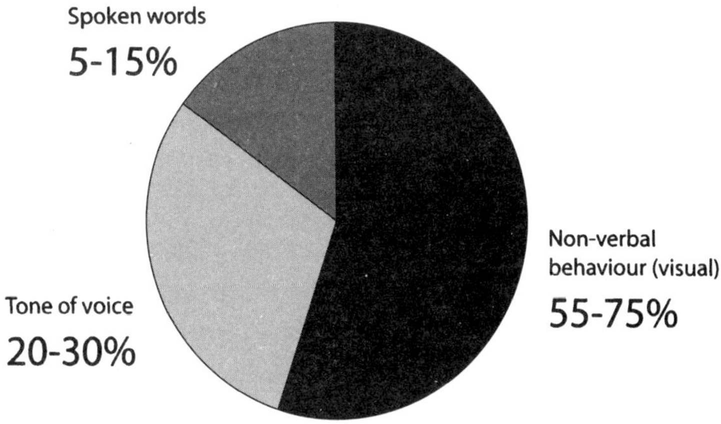

Impact of Communication (Whole Body Language)

You can see from this breakdown why the impact of an email is less than that of a phone call, which in turn is much less than that of a face to face conversation. This is why you should always use the face to face methodology to communicate the most important messages. It's a lesson that fax and telesales people would do well to learn.

You can see all this in action in the context of getting to know a business acquaintance. The style of an initial email gives you some idea of the correspondent's operational drivers; a later telephone conversation will add an element of personality to the picture you are building; but your view and understanding of that person only comes together when you meet them in the flesh.

To be conscious of one's body language to the extent that you should use it most profitably to influence is therefore vital. Here are a few critical things to be aware of:

1. **Eye contact**. If you do nothing else to improve your body language, make sure your eye contact is good. The eyes say it all – you can read a message from the eyes without anything else happening. Eye contact should take place when speaking or listening because these two activities form part

of the communication process. It is not necessary when thinking because thinking is an internal activity. So, you ask a question and the other side listens (eye contact); the other side thinks about their answer (no eye contact) – notice how very often their gaze moves toward the upper left of their vision field; the other side gives you an answer (eye contact).

Beware holding a direct gaze for too long. Six seconds (a relatively long time) is generally thought to be the maximum period. Any longer and the other side will begin to think that at best you are over assertive, at worst psychotic. Extend the six seconds by removing the immediacy of the gaze from the eyes to other areas of the face – chin, forehead, nose. There will still appear to be good eye contact, but the potentially threatening glare has disappeared.

Poor eye contact gives the impression of shiftiness, dishonesty and fear.

2. **Body posture**. There are many things to think about here. Here are one or two of the more important:

    - *Handshakes* should be nicely firm accompanied by eye contact. A hand cruncher is an indicator of a lack of self-confidence manifested in a need to dominate; a wet fish shows either a weak personality or a lack of interest in you. Avoid both.

    - Always adopt an *open body posture* – arms relaxed at your side with hands out turned. This shows that you are approachable and ready to talk openly and honestly. Conversely, do not wrap yourself up by giving yourself a big hug or generally tensing your body. This indicates that you feel you are falling apart and gives out a 'wish I was somewhere else' message.

    - When sitting to converse, *lean forward a little* with the head at a slight angle. This is a great listening posture and shows the other side that you are interested in what they are saying. On the contrary, do not lean back with your hands clasped behind your head. This denotes arrogance, superiority and boredom – definitely not good for successful influencing.

- *Smile when appropriate,* but don't overdo it. There is nothing worse that a smile at the wrong time or an overblown inane grin. Both are indicators of nervousness and being uncomfortable with the interaction.

8.7 I understand that assertiveness is one of the key skills required to influence effectively, but am not sure exactly what it is. How do I know if I am being assertive and what are the key characteristics I should consciously be developing?

Assertiveness is the form of behaviour which we need to adopt if we are to deal effectively with other people. It should be distinguished from aggressive behaviour (with which it is often confused) and passive behaviour which are at the extremes of the behaviour spectrum. The spectrum looks like this:

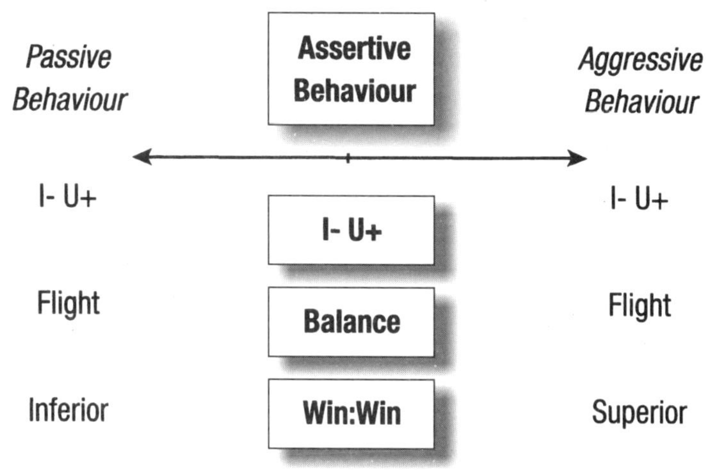

Behaviour Continuum

Let's put the extremes to rest before tackling the positive:

1. **Aggressive behaviour**. You are more likely to understand what this is. It is behaviour which involves bullying, controlling, humiliating, belittling, ignoring and dismissing other people. The aggressive manager behaves in this way because he lacks self-confidence and needs to feel superior. He believes he can only gain respect though political manipulation and a psychologically overbearing approach towards his team members. He thinks that he is an ok guy (I+), and you are nothing (U -). The outcome of any interaction with him is that he wins and you lose. Needless to say, this form of behaviour in a leader is the antithesis of good communication and influencing practice, is stressful, demotivates and is generally totally unacceptable. The organization which employs someone who consistently manages in this way and is impervious to personal change should ask itself whether that person is the right fit for that organization's vision of itself.

Examples

1. X is leaving work at the end of tiring day. His manager waylays him as X is about to quit the building and asks him to return and do an urgent task now. X declines to stay, to which the manager responds that his performance review and potential promotion will be in jeopardy if he does not.

2. Y suddenly comes up against a crisis over an important client account about which he needs the help of a particular colleague. The colleague is just leaving for another meeting and X anxiously asks when he will be back. The colleague responds: 'That's none of your business.'

2. **Passive behaviour**. This form of behaviour is at the other end of the spectrum, but arises often for the same reason – lack of self-confidence. Passive people fail to stand up for themselves. They are apologetic, diffident and self-effacing. They exude ambiguity, usually failing to express themselves honestly. They are often the wallflowers in open discussions, retreating into silence rather than participate. The passive person thinks you are great (U +), but that he is worthless (I -). He expects the outcome of any discussion to be a victory for you and a defeat for him. Trying to pin him down is like trying to nail jelly to the ceiling. Passive behaviour can be extremely disruptive, causing negative vibes and frustrations within the team. It is unlikely that a people manager manifesting passive behaviour will, without a commitment to behavioural change, last long since he will be unable to demonstrate true leadership skills. In particular, you cannot communicate with silence.

Examples

1. Z is invited by a colleague to go for a drink after work and asked which bar he would prefer. Z says: 'I don't mind.' The bar which the colleague suggests to Z is a smoky sleazy dive which Z does not like, but Z responds: 'OK then.'

2. B is praised by his manager for the successful completion of a project. B sheepishly responds: 'It was nothing. It's what I'm paid to do.'

3. **Assertive behaviour**. Right in the middle of the spectrum, this is the form of behaviour to which not only all people managers should be aiming to aspire, but every single human being in his dealings with his fellows. Assertiveness involves expressing yourself in a direct, honest and open way. It

entails being straightforward and fearless in stating your views and encouraging the person with whom you are dealing to do the same (if they are not already assertive themselves – and some of your team may not be). In particular, it enables you, in the best possible fashion, to say 'No'. Not only does this give you a sense of self-respect and self-esteem, but says that this is also the right form of behaviour for the other side. The result is that conversations are able to state views clearly, lay all cards on the table, recognize problems, discuss solutions and agree progress. In other words, you end up in true negotiating fashion with win-win. Both sides are saying to each other: I'm OK (I+) and you are also OK (U+).

Examples

1. *C invites D to attend a client conference where D's specialist input will be helpful. D agrees to come but then fails to turn up. Later, C rings D and says: 'D, I understood you were coming to the meeting. It would have been helpful for you to have been there. What happened?'*

2. *You are having a very busy day. F, a junior colleague, asks for your help with a particular task. You reply: 'Happy to help out, F, but can it wait for a couple of hours until things quieten down for me?'*

To help with developing your assertiveness, here are some **practical tips**:

- *Make statements that are clear and honest.* Use the word 'I' confidently.
- *Eliminate uncertainty* by letting people know what you want. Take the initiative to provide all relevant information.

- *Be specific and succinct.* Use a short, pithy sentence to express your view.
- *Be positive.* Talk about what you want or need. Avoid vagueness and negativity.
- *Ask for the possible.* Be realistic in your demands to avoid frustration and resistance.
- *Make only genuine requests.* If there is only one solution, state exactly what you want.
- *Respect others' opinions.* Avoid being dismissive or contemptuous.
- *Respond to others' requests honestly.* Take time out to think or research if necessary.

By utilizing this approach and developing these skills, you will find that your conversations and communication generally becomes productive, demands respect, influences and concludes with getting by and large what you want.

As a back up tool to assist with understanding aggressive, assertive and passive behaviour in practice, consider the **Transactional Analysis** (TA) psychological model. TA takes the view that the three forms of behaviour that we manifest are that of the *parent*, the *child* and the *adult*. The parent and child forms of behaviour are regressive, having been learnt during our formative years and, for those who behave in these ways, have not been abandoned during our maturing process for the more adult approach to communication. In a nutshell, the child throws the rattle out of its pram, the parent admonishes the child for its bad behaviour, but the adult looks objectively and calmly at the situation and responds with positive suggestions and actions.

Adult behaviour can be readily linked to assertive behaviour. Parent and child behaviour, however, can both be either aggressive or passive. For example, road rage is aggressive but is clearly childish; equally, passive silence may be a behavioural technique for the admonishing parent.

The TA theory is that when we are met by childish or parental behaviour, there is a subconscious tendency to respond with the opposite behaviour. So parental behaviour induces a childish response; childish behaviour produces a parental response. The way out of this destructive circle is to consciously and unemotionally respond as an adult. The other side then discovers that to continue in the childish or parental vein is impossible and is drawn themselves, whether they like it or not, into an adult response and therefore a civilized approach to sorting out the problem.

Example

M is in one of two lunchtime queues at the office canteen. The cashier at the head of M's queue is trying to deal with a number of people ahead of M. M turns round to N standing behind him and says: 'Aren't they slow here. I always seem to get in the wrong queue.'

The impatience manifested here is childish behaviour, and it is easier to analyze the above example in this way rather than look at the aggressive/passive distinction. A parental response from N might be: 'Do stop complaining and just wait your turn.' An adult response from N might go something like: 'Yes, queues can be frustrating at times, but there isn't much we can do about it today, so let's just hang in there. It won't be long.'

8.8 One of the aims of influencing is to persuade the other side to accept your point of view. Are there any techniques which will assist me with the process of persuading? How could I use these effectively?

Apart from general sales techniques, which are outside the scope of this book, there is one particular model around which you might structure a conversation. In addition, you might use one of the various forms of power available to you as a people manager to help you on your way. Let's look at each of these suggestions in turn.

1. A model for a holding a persuasive conversation

This model is known as the 8 Ps of Persuasion. It follows an eight stage process, memorable since they all begin with the letter P, on which you can structure an effective influencing conversation.

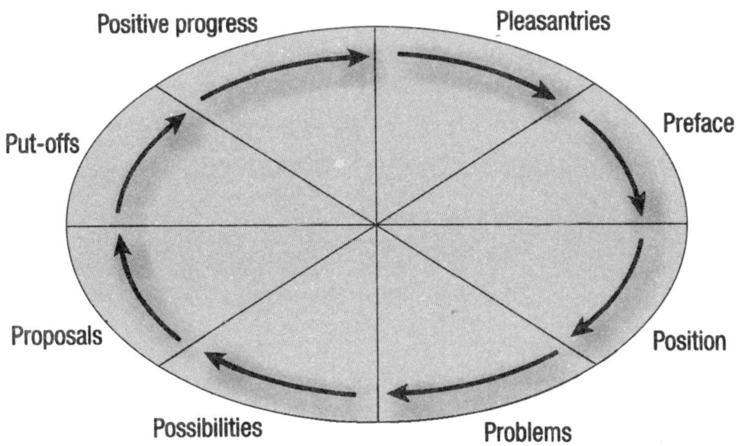

Developing a Persuasive Strategy – the 8 'Ps' of Constructing a Conversation

Here are the stages, moving from the one o'clock clockwise, and how they work:

- *Stage 1 – Pleasantries.* Never simply dive in the deep end with an important conversation. Begin by asking how the other person is, whether they had a good weekend, how the children are etc. This relaxes the atmosphere and shows that you are there to reach a shared agreement developed in a cordial atmosphere. Do not, however, allow this stage to go on for too long. There is business to do!

- *Stage 2 – Preface.* Begin formally by stating why you are meeting and what the key issues are. This allows both sides to see the big picture surrounding the conversation and enables them to see their points of view in the broad context of desired outcomes.

- *Stage 3 – Position.* Each person states his position on the key issues to be resolved. This enables each side not only to see but also to understand the various angles and approaches to achieving the end result. It will make detailed discussion of potential solutions easier.

- *Stage 4 – Problems.* Here you consider the negative aspects of the matter under discussion – what the difficulties are with each side's approach, what practical issues may arise that could make a solution difficult. These negatives are important to bear in mind when considering the workability of the ultimate solution.

- *Stage 5 – Possibilities.* Now move from the negative to the positive. What are the potential solutions, what are the advantages and disadvantages of each, how would the alternatives satisfy each side's position? It is important at this stage to table all potential solutions.

- *Stage 6 – Proposal.* Having analyzed all potential solutions, it is now time to pick one as a proposal for moving forward. Clearly, you need to choose one which on the face of it is acceptable to – and will work for – both sides.
- *Stage 7 – Put-offs.* Rigorously work through the proposal looking out for implementation difficulties, outcomes which even at this stage may be unacceptable to one side, or other issues likely to cause problems in achieving the solution. If you discover any real hindrances to progress, go back to stage 6 and come up with an alternative proposal.
- *Stage 8 – Positive action.* Once you have done the deal, you can breathe a sigh of relief, but not before agreeing the implementation process, next steps and by who and a timetable for making things happen.

You might even add a ninth stage – praise – when you can pat each other on the back for a job well done and maybe celebrate. Either way, the use of this Ps model will help you, via a structured process, to achieve a positive outcome to the problem you sat down to resolve.

2. Persuasive power and its use

The word 'power' has less than positive connotations at a time when, in the democratic world at least, people, including your team members, are demanding more and more of a say in the decision making that affects their lives including their working lives. Nevertheless, used in the right context and the right way, power is important for a leader as an aid to persuading people to help get things done.

Hersey and Blanchard's research led them to conclude that there are seven different types of power a leader can wield in order to assist him in the influencing process. The use of these types of power tends to correlate with the level of maturity of a team member and, hence, the leadership style which you as a people manager can be expected to adopt towards that individual. Here are those seven *'Levers of Power'* and the situations in which you might be expected to utilize them:

- *Coercive power.* Here the leader tells people what to do. You would use it with new and junior members of staff who are unfamiliar with processes and lack experience and knowledge.

- *Connection power.* Here you influence through whom you know in the organization's hierarchy. The power stems from the other side not wanting to rock the establishment boat. This type of influencing works well with relatively junior team members.

- *Reward power.* Moderately experienced team members are willing to experiment, and the carrot they need to do so is some form of motivational reward on conclusion of the project. The leader is perceived to be able to provide that reward, whether in a material, career development or other acceptable form.

- *Legitimate power.* Here the leader influences through his position in the organizational hierarchy. Moderately experienced team members are able to accept the leader and his status simply by virtue of his being the team's leader.

- *Personal power.* Sometimes known as referent power, the leader here uses his personality and relationship building capabilities when working with individual team members. By using this form of power, the leader provides encouragement and instils confidence by influencing at a one to one level. The team member responds by liking and admiring his manager.

- *Information power.* Here the team member relies on the leader to provide information and background knowledge in order for him to improve performance. The leader makes himself available to clarify or explain issues, and the more experienced team member is happy to get things done through that informational support.

- *Expert power*. For the most experienced team members, where delegation and empowerment are the norm, the leader influences by manifesting the leadership and facilitation expertise that allows the team member to be self reliant, and commands respect from the team member because of those skills.

So, as a people manager, think about how you might best use these types of power to help with the communication and influencing process both within your team and in your relationships with the rest of your organization.

3. Personal power in the 21st century organization

In the age of empowerment and trust, the last three of the seven levers above become critically important. In particular, the personality of the leader (and hence his personal power) is a crucial factor in a people manager's success.

Personal power is said to derive from two elements: the **attractiveness** of the leader as a person, i.e. is he likeable, and the **charisma** that flows out from the personality itself. If you are both attractive and charismatic as a leader, the world is your oyster. If you are charismatic but unattractive, you may well be one of the rather nastier dictators which the world unfortunately sees from time to time. Idi Amin and Pol Pot come immediately to mind. If, on other hand, you are an attractive person but lack charisma, all is not lost if you adopt the traits which in the present world are perceived by team members as those which demand respect and support.

Before dealing with these personal power traits, it should be said that we cannot all be charismatic. Charisma is intangible; we recognize it when we see it and we know when it is lacking. It takes a variety of forms and can manifest itself both in a more extroverted as well as a quieter manner. But where it does exist, in whatever form, its characteristics are clear – it effortlessly demands respect, loyalty and followership, and influences accordingly.

So if, as a people manager, you understand that you are not the most charismatic person in the world, don't despair, but rather rely on the fact that you are in any event a likable person, and develop and use assertively the following key traits that are essential influencing factors for successful leaders in the current world:

- *Energy*. Develop endurance and stamina. You can do this by keeping fit and generally adopting a healthy lifestyle. It also helps if you like and are committed to your job. The resulting energy which you manifest in executing your managerial role will be respected by the team and other colleagues alike.
- *Focus*. Don't allow this energy to be dissipated too thinly across too many projects or by concentrating on too much detail. Concentrate on big picture objectives and deal with each of them in turn, managing the team and the detail accordingly. This sort of focus shows determination and commitment to achievement.
- *Flexibility*. We live in a world of constant change. What may have been a sound objective six months ago may now have been superseded by events. Equally, the strategy for implementing a particular objective may no longer be realistic. Whatever the problem, do not stick rigidly to plans but be prepared to work round, adapt and modify as necessary. Develop emotional detachment and refuse to be sucked in to the 'it's my baby' syndrome. This sort of positive flexibility accommodates differing interests and thus creates broad support.
- *Toughness*. We are not talking here about physical strength but inner toughness. It involves the combination of being assertive where necessary, following through an argument when you are convinced of the rightness of your view and taking and recovering from knocks and setbacks quickly. If you stand up for your team and what it is seeking to achieve by strongly fighting your corner, this will further add to the respect and trust the team has for you.

- **Sensitivity.** Emotional intelligence is a fashionable managerial trait at the start of this century. What it essentially involves is the ability to read and understand other people, to be able to lock into their needs and to take their viewpoint into account when decision making. Generally speaking, women are inherently good at this; men need to work at it. There is no doubt that if you learn to practise this skill, the respect you gain as a result of increased inter-personal sensitivity will be enormous.
- **Humility.** Sometimes we all suffer from an over inflated ego which tells us that we are right and everyone else is wrong. Think – is this sort of behaviour a problem for you? If so, try to sublimate it for the sake of building networks, friendships and generally getting along with others. Acknowledge good ideas and success in your team, particularly where your own approach has proved mistaken. Most importantly, be big enough to be able sometimes to say: 'I'm sorry. I was wrong.' It is amazing how much understanding and support this manifestation of human failure generates.

By demonstrating these six traits, your personal power will increase. Add the standard measures of likeability – humour, enthusiasm, confidence and commitment – and your leadership influencing skills will grow apace irrespective of the level of charisma you naturally generate.

8.9 I am never very confident that I make a real impact when I am presenting my views and hoping to influence my team or colleagues. What can I do to ensure that my views are heard and respected?

Impact is closely aligned to the image you present when working face to face with another person or people. This image is a critical part of the influencing process and, within the context of your personality, needs to be developed. If you do, then when you present your views to your colleagues they are impressed and therefore influenced by the impact of your self-presentation style. So, what in particular should you be conscious of in this context of image and impact building? There are four matters for you to consider:

1. **Your personality.** You cannot change this, but you can ensure that who you are comes across. Know yourself, then be yourself. It takes some time to do this naturally. It involves a loss of self-consciousness borne of the development of self-confidence. We are all different, but we respect and recognize each other by virtue of who we are and how we manage the interaction of our differences. So remove any mask that hides the real you; relax and be yourself.

2. **How you look.** We live in a society which unfortunately tends to judge people by their appearance. I use the word 'unfortunately' because you can readily change your appearance in order to fool others as to who you really are. The superficiality of your appearance can detract from an understanding of the inner you. So-called 'power dressing' is an example of presenting an image of authority which may not in reality be warranted. So the general rule must be to dress, shave, make-up, style your hair etc in a way with which you feel most comfortable. This will send out the best possible message that your appearance and who you are do actually coincide. Image consultants nowadays have the means to help to make this happen.

   Having said that, there are clearly social and work related ground rules that determine dress codes and appearance norms which you must follow if you are to be an influential member of 'the club'. At work, is the business suit the usual attire or something more casual? Do you have dress-down days when casual dress is the norm? The answer to these questions will determine what image you should generally present in the workplace. Apart from this, learn quickly the rules of attire for any special situation. If in doubt, dress up. There is nothing worse than turning up in a rugby shirt to a black tie event; the reverse situation however, whilst initially awkward, can be carried off with panache. Whatever you wear, always look smart and well turned out. People are turned off by a sloppy appearance.

3. **Influencing skills.** Ensure that the 7 Deadly Skills (of which, of course, this is one) are all working effectively. In particular, ask incisive questions, listen proactively and attentively, use good body language and put across your views assertively. The very use of these skills is impressive in its own right.

4. **Presentation skills.** We are not talking here solely about techniques for standing up and delivering a formal presentation. What follows equally applies to holding a one to one conversation in an informal setting. Here are some tips to help create an impact:

   - *Speak slowly.* Our brains work significantly faster than our tongues, and if our thought process is too far ahead of our spoken delivery, we begin to stumble over our words and lose the train of thought because we are continually failing to catch up with ourselves. Equally, the person to whom we are speaking has to spend time absorbing and analyzing our message. If our words are tumbling out at a rate of knots, their understanding is going to become a difficulty and we become unreasonably frustrated that what we have said has not been taken in first time.

   - *Enunciate clearly.* Don't mumble into your beard. Make sure that the other side has the best opportunity to use their listening skills effectively. Open your mouth and allow the words to come out clearly. Mumbling is a classic sign of either disinterest, a lack of assertiveness or being economical with the truth. This principle is particularly important when you have a strong accent to which other ears are not necessarily attuned. Modulating your tone of voice also helps with understanding, but remember to stress the important words. For example, avoid the trend, prevalent in some media quarters, of stressing auxiliary verbs such as 'are' 'will' and 'were' which mean nothing in themselves. And, at the end of sentences, try to hit the median between tailing off badly and rising to a high pitched sing-song.

- *Breathe regularly and deeply.* When communicating and influencing, we are often understandably somewhat tense and nervous. This is reflected in shallow breathing and a possibly shakier and higher pitched voice that we would normally employ when relaxed. Counteract this by taking a deep breath at the beginning of each sentence. Deep breathing slows everything down and helps us to relax. We then speak more clearly, more confidently and with greater authority.

8.10 A significant element of successful influencing must involve developing a solid personal understanding between me and the person with whom I'm communicating. Are there any tips for helping to cement this understanding?

The seventh and final Deadly Sin really sums up all the others. What you are seeking to achieve by developing and using these skills is a solid rapport with the other side. Once you have that rapport, agreement, decision making and progress become much more straightforward.

Rapport is about meeting people on their own level and making them feel at home with you. It demonstrates the oneness between you and the other side in what you both say and do. It seeks to emphasize the similarities between you rather than the differences, and it creates empathy and understanding in the relationship.

As we have seen, it is a truism that there are some people in life whom we like and respond to better than others. Rapport comes easily with those we like, but how do we develop it with those who do not seem so easy to get on with? The answer lies in using a technique know as mirroring.

Mirroring involves adopting the behaviour and approach of the other side so that it appears that they are seeing a mirror image of themselves in the way you are acting. This makes them not only feel comfortable, but also generates a belief that this person opposite understands them. If both sides consciously undertake mirroring, then the likelihood of the development of genuine rapport is extremely high.

So, in what practical ways can mirroring work? Here are some examples:

- *Speech*. Try to copy the speed, tone, volume and pitch of the other side's voice. Make a speedy assessment of the other's vocabulary – choice of words, any professional terminology or jargon. Use all these to make the other side feel comfortable and that you are, literally, speaking the same language.

- *Feelings/outlook*. Attempt to lock in quickly to the other side's mood. Are they having a bad day? If so, mirror that sense of despondency or frustration. Discover what their attitude or beliefs are about key issues and sympathize with those views. How enthusiastic or tolerant are they regarding the matters under discussion? To what extent do they wish to get involved? Take a similar stance yourself and watch the other side relax, drop their mask and start to think 'I can do business with this person'.

- *Body language*. In some ways, this is the easiest mirroring activity. Simply watch the other side, then subtly mimic their sitting position, facial expressions and body movements. The subconscious effect on them is dramatic – they start to feel at one with you without really knowing why. If possible, extend this mirroring to dress – suit to suit, jeans to jeans and so on – anything to help make the other side feel more comfortable in their dealings with you.

Example

Next time you find yourself in an informal meeting, observe the body posture of a colleague sitting close by. Copy that posture, then a few minutes later consciously change your posture at an appropriate point in the discussion. Wait until a fairly quiet and relaxed moment to make your change, then watch your colleague shift their position to mirror yours. He will not even be aware that he is doing it. This should cause you if no one else a certain amount of amusement!

So what is the result of successful rapport building? Two states of affairs arise. Firstly, you gain **credibility**. By showing that you understand how the other side ticks, you comprehend the other side's needs, appear totally competent and in control of what you are doing and are better able to help them find a mutually acceptable outcome to the issue under discussion. Secondly, you have gained their **trust and confidence**. Your genuine interest in the other side's position allows them to feel safe in discussing issues sensitive to them, whilst at the same time allowing them the respect they need to retain control over their own decision making.

Summary

Here is a summary of some practical tips and techniques to help you with your communication skills:

- Build relationships with colleagues that go beyond the rational and include the emotional. Expressing feelings in a conversation adds to understanding and positive outcomes.
- Be aware of the different communication vehicles available to you and select the right medium for the right message. In particular, important messages require a face to face interaction.
- We communicate to influence. Remember to use the 'seven deadly skills' to best advantage and so enhance your influencing capability.
- Ask incisive questions. Use open and closed questions as appropriate, but avoid those such as leading questions, which are likely to result in an ambiguous answer.
- Listen proactively. Use maximum effort and energy to focus on what other people are saying to you. Of all the influencing skills, being a good listener is arguably the most critical.
- Use appropriate body language. Keep good eye contact and avoid negative or unhelpful body postures.
- Be assertive in your interactions with others. Say what you mean clearly and confidently. Avoid aggressive or passive behaviour.
- Structure conversations to maximize their persuasive effect. Use whatever persuasive power you have wisely and constructively and openly manifest the personal traits of the influential leader.
- Be aware of your image and the impact this has on others. Look competent, dress appropriately and present what you have to say clearly and coherently.

- Above all, develop a sense of rapport with the person you are dealing with. Use mirroring techniques to make people comfortable when conversing with you and to generate greater interpersonal understanding.

NINE
Change management

9.1 There are major changes afoot with my department and they will impact strongly on my team. What are the key issues I should be thinking about in setting out to manage these changes effectively?

As we saw earlier, change is a natural element in human existence. Nothing stays the same for ever. In personal terms, your move to becoming a people manager was a major change event. The change on this occasion is one which affects your team, and you have to handle it effectively.

Change management is one of the key skills that people managers need to develop in a permanently fluctuating business world, and the most difficult problem for you is carrying the members of your team with you. This is because they, like you, have an emotional response to change and all of them must be managed through the change curve. Since you have already been through that process (see Chapter 1), you now have some inner understanding and wisdom to help your team members along the same sort of road.

The first issues to deal with, however, are to ask *what and why change is taking place and who is instigating it*, since your approach to managing the change will vary depending on the answers.

1. **Externally driven change**. Examples of this will include increased expectations and demands from customers or clients, the introduction of new technologies or perhaps a change in demographics which affects product demand or the composition of your workforce.

2. **Internally driven change**. Under this heading, you could include budget cuts and their effect, squeezed resources to cope with a sudden increase in demand, reorganization from line to matrix working, departmental integration and other mergers or a cultural change towards a more empowered workforce.

In the case of *externally driven change and internal change driven by senior management*, you will have been forewarned of what was to come via the information cascade which ultimately reached you from your line manager. In terms of managing the process, your approach will be 'we're all in this together', since as team manager you will need psychologically as well as practically to adapt to the change in exactly the same way as your team members.

If, on the other hand, *internal change is driven locally by you*, e.g. team reorganization, physical relocation etc, you have a positive advantage since you are already committed, and you can concentrate your energies on supporting your team members through the process.

If you recognize this difference, the way you approach the change process can be modified to suit the particular change situation, and the likelihood of failure is significantly reduced.

9.2 My observation tells me that many change initiatives either fail or do not have outcomes as successful as they should be. Why is this?

There are a variety of reasons why change programmes are less than successful. Here are some of them. Be on the lookout and avoid them like the plague if they start to intrude on your own change process.

- *Being too complacent*. Change is hard work. It does not happen by itself. In particular, do not suppose that once you have set the ball rolling, everything else will happen automatically.

- *Too little teamwork.* You must involve your team and supportive outsiders to help guide the change process through. Trying to work alone is asking for trouble.

- *Lack of self-confidence in achieving the change outcome.* The change initiative will have been created through a vision of a better way of doing things. Do not lose sight of that vision. It is a powerful driver.

- *Poor communication.* Trying to do things differently without keeping people informed is playing with fire. People will not support you if they do not know what is going on.

- *Allowing obstacles to block the path.* Problems, sometimes major ones, will always arise during the course of the change process. Do not become disheartened and give up because of them.

- *Failing to create clear milestones.* Major change cannot be achieved all at once. If you do not breakdown the steps and generate short term wins, everyone will become disenchanted.

- *Neglecting to embed changes in your organization's culture.* Your change must become part 'of the way we do things around here'. If you fail to sell it effectively across your business, no one will take notice of it.

Case study

Company X and Company Y were both website designer operations with a host of high profile clients. They recognized the synergy between their business and the potential cost savings if they were to merge – and merge they did. After the merger, it soon became clear that there were problems. Here is a summary of what emerged when the two attempted to start working together.

COMPANY X	COMPANY Y
• operations driven	• marketing driven
• line management structure	• matrix management structure
• left brain thinking	• right brain thinking
• task oriented	• people oriented
• focus on collectivism/teams	• focus on individuality
• office in East London	• office in West London

Whatever the synergy and cost savings, it was clear that culturally the two companies were poles apart, and for chalk to work effectively with cheese a major change programme would need to be implemented. However, the changes necessitated by the merger had not been thought through during the due diligence stage and no comprehensive plan of action was in place to try to overcome the problems via a systematic and staged process. The merger was an operational failure and within three months any attempt at integration was abandoned.

Having got rid of a few negatives, you can now look forward positively to change management success through utilizing **three key tools**:

- your own change leadership skills
- implementing a logical change process
- your people management skills.

These are the next issues on your change agenda.

9.3 As a people manager seeking to implement change, what key skills should I be developing and utilizing to see the change process through?

Quite apart from the general people management skills which we have been discussing already, there are a number of key leadership traits which you should seek to acquire and use to ensure a successful outcome to the change process.

You can call these the **Change Leadership Dozen**, since there are 12 of them to develop. Here they are in no particular order:

1. **Maintaining a clear vision.** Change requires a clear intention to act and a helicopter view of how the future will look. Your vision needs to be consistent, with each facet of change supporting rather than conflicting with the others. You must have the desired outcomes in your mind's eye. You need to be clear about what needs to be done.

2. **Competence at project management.** Whether the change is large or small, the change leader brings top class project management and coordination skills to bear on the process. This is all about being able to run people, systems and information to achieve the end result. You need to be a superb organizer.

3. **Analytical rigour.** Great change managers dig deep into the root causes of situations and think through all the elements required to reach a good decision. They are committed to a full examination of all relevant information. You therefore need to be able to get to the heart of the matter.

4. **Definition of problems.** Difficulties are endemic in change programmes. You need to be able to uncover these and keep them under control. Problematic matters must be kept within sensible boundaries. Alongside logic, intuition is often a useful tool to have for identifying and weighing up the often multiple causes of complex problems.

5. **Structured approach to problem solving.** You will wish to use a set methodology to understand how problems may be affecting the change process, what possible solutions present themselves and which one will work best. This skill is vital if the overall vision is to be turned into reality. Here, you need to be highly disciplined.

6. **Building support.** You need to be able to create a critical mass of support to ease the passage of the change programme. This will comprise a group of like minded people to act as the resource to help get things done. You should thus be able to acquire those resources to drive the programme forward.

7. **Communicating persuasively.** Here you need to use to maximum advantage the whole range of influencing skills you have developed in a different context. These will help you convey your ideas, values and strategies. You will need a combination of rational logic and a heartfelt desire to effect change. In particular, use your magnetic personality – your charisma and attractiveness.

8. **Openness to criticism.** Debate and feedback are essential to gather data, sharpen opinions and test ideas. Good change leaders welcome this and use their listening skills to absorb differing opinions so that they implement the best change using the best process. You will accept criticism where your own idea has proved inadequate without defensiveness or loss of face. You are open and responsive.

9. **Resilience and willpower.** You will encounter setback and difficulties, especially from those resistant to change. You must react to these without losing sight of the end goal. Mix endurance, tenacity and persistence with subtlety. Prove yourself to be made of steel.

10. **Failure as a learning curve.** We all make mistakes, and the change leader is no exception. The key thing here is to learn from the mistake and ensure it does not happen again.

Resolve and determination are enhanced when errors are analyzed. You should review setbacks with others, then move forward again incorporating the lessons learnt into the change plan.

11. **Dealing with uncertainty.** This means coping with change within change. No plan ever runs totally smoothly. You need to feel comfortable in uncertain situations, able to cope with the unpredictable and ride the whirlwind whilst maintaining control. In a phrase, you will be calm in the crises which inevitably arise during the change management process.

12. **Resistance to overload.** Energy and vitality are critical weapons in a change leader's armoury. It is important therefore that you maintain these traits by not allowing yourself to become overburdened by taking on too much, becoming stressed and losing sight of the big picture. Delegate all detail as a matter of course, and retain a clear head for real decision making.

Spend time developing the Change Leadership Dozen, and watch your star rise as you engender the respect and support necessary to see change through.

9.4 So, I now know what change leadership skills I need to utilize, but what sort of structured process should I follow to ensure a change transition that is a smooth as possible?

As usual, there has to be an element of flexibility here, but subject to your keeping this permanently at the front of your mind, here is a process which will help you see things through.

1. **Firm up on your vision.** Be clear on the sort of change you are looking for. Create a picture in your mind of how things will look once the change has gone through. Focus on the future and the new opportunities that will be created, and begin to shape your current day to day thinking with these in mind.

2. **Create a strategy.** Use SWOT analysis to provide you with:
   - the strengths of the change you are envisaging
   - the weaknesses under the present system that will be eliminated and those you will ensure do not occur under the new regime
   - the opportunities provided under the changed scenario for improved team and company wide performance
   - the threats to the team and possibly other areas of the business which you need to handle.

3. **Plan, Plan, Plan.** You now move to a detailed list of actions that will form the operational basis of the change process. It cannot be stressed enough that every productive minute spent on planning is worth its weight in gold. You should in effect treat the change management as a project. To have a plan to refer to is essential if everything is to happen as you have envisaged. Break down all the stages and tasks that must happen, then use a GANTT chart or similar to give you a visual presentation of the process. This should contain key objectives, sub targets and milestones to be achieved along the route in chronological order.

Here is an example of a **C**(apability) **O**(peration) **R**(eadiness) **T**(imescale) chart, which is one example of visual mapping you might use.

Key objectives and sub-targets	Timescale Date for completion	Capability			Readiness			Implemented and operational
		H	M	L	H	M	L	
1a (s-t)		✔				✔		
1b (s-t)			✔			✔		
1c (s-t)*				✔				
1 (ob)								
✔				✔		2a		
	✔			✔		2b		
✔				✔		etc		

** = high need to resolve capability issue*

4. **Communicate, communicate, communicate**. You cannot talk to people too much during the change process.
   - Talk to *colleagues external to the team.* What you are proposing to do may well have been driven by external factors, or at least will have needed the approval of your line manager. Thus, this element of communication must come first. Your stakeholder analysis and communication strategy will help here. Apart from your line manager, is there anyone whose approval you might need formally or informally? Who on the matrix will require handling particularly sensitively? Who might have ideas for implementation which could be really helpful? Who might be able to open doors that would

otherwise remain closed? Maximize the networking opportunities that your plan for change throws up.

- Prepare your *team*. Consult them at the earliest opportunity to obtain buy-in and to pre-empt resistance. It is vital that they hear nothing by way of rumour. Back-handed information is a sure route to anxiety and a lack of commitment. This could be a problem since your chats outside the team might have produced leaks. Manage those with swift action.

  Talk to the team about the vision, strategy and plan; in particular timescales. Let them know that you will be talking to each team member individually to discuss their role in the process. Do not start these talks for at least one week after the plenary session in order to allow the idea of change to sink in. As the change process continues, remember to encourage ongoing discussion, listen, be prepared to accept positive feedback and use your influencing skills to maximum effect.

5. **Set up monitoring systems**. These need to check regular progress in four areas: people, resources, timescales and procedures.

   - *People*. Use your delegation skills here to ensure that the right people are doing the right things after a full briefing. Then monitor their progress as appropriate.

   - *Resources*. Are the right supportive pieces of kit, external consultants, budget monies etc all happening according to plan? Keep a regular eye on external help to ensure that it all happens when it should.

   - *Timescales*. Refer to your CORT or GANTT chart to check that everything is on course for hitting the right deadlines and that any slippage can be rectified. It may be that the changes you are bringing about are designed to be implemented for action on a specific unalterable date. Make timescales generous to avoid these potential difficulties.

- *Procedures*. Make these as straightforward as possible. Remember the (rather arrogant) acronym KISS – keep it simple stupid! In particular, ensure that all instructions eliminate unnecessary information, and don't use jargon.

And finally, avoid complacency ('my process is perfect – nothing can go wrong'). Always be conscious of the potential for unpredictability.

9.5 As a people manager, my greatest concern is how to win over my team members to accept the changes that I wish to implement. There will always be some who are less enthusiastic than others. How do I win all of my team over to the new way of doing things?

Behaviour varies from team member to team member when change is in the air. This is because change affects different personalities in different ways. Some people feel insecure when change is imminent; others dislike change which they do not control; others yet again feel that their lives are going nowhere without more or less permanent change to stimulate them.

Here is a model which divides people into three general categories which reflect their attitude to change. These are the **functionals**, the **non-functionals** and the **dis-functionals** and you will find examples of each within your own team.

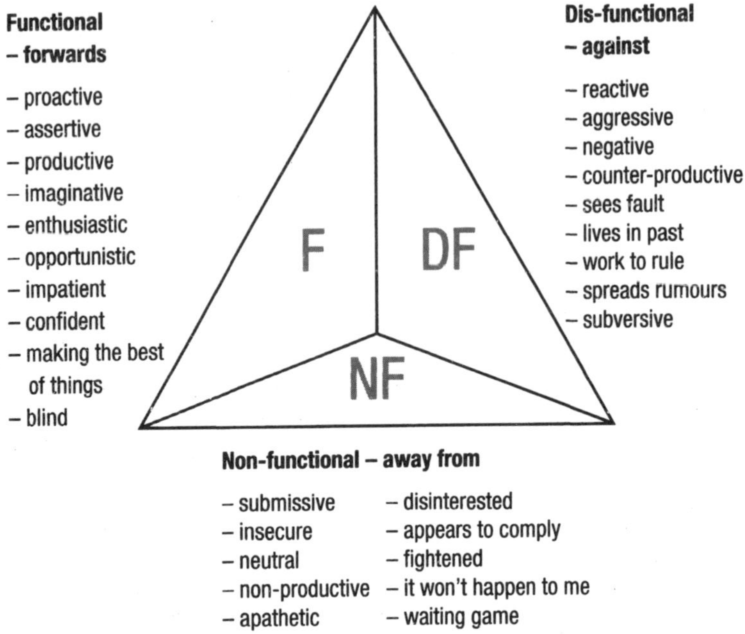

The Change Orientation Model

The diagram above can be summarized as follows:

- *Category 1 – Functionals.* These are your team members who welcome the change. On hearing of the moves afoot, their reaction is 'let's go for it'. They will be supportive of you and will be keen to face up to the challenges and the difficulties ahead. The downside is that their enthusiasm may get the better of them, making them blind to the realities of the change scenario. They nevertheless are your key allies.

- *Category 2 – Dis-functionals.* Here you have team members who hate the notion of change whether for rational or irrational reasons. Their position is to become entrenched in their behaviour which works to sabotage the changes you are introducing. Their negativity is proactive and may involve not only a positive refusal to cooperate but even outright subversiveness.

- *Category 3 – Non-functionals.* This group within your team simply refuses to understand that change is taking place. They are frightened at the prospect and retreat into themselves. They stick their heads in the sand and try to believe that nothing is different and that they will eventually wake up as if from a bad dream. Their general approach may take the form of apathy or indifference.

The question remains: how do you handle and deal with each of these types so that eventually the whole team is on board and committed to the new way of doing things?

Here is a three pronged approach for getting everybody to accept the change:

1. **Talk to each team member individually** to discover how they feel about the changes and to determine into which of the three categories each falls. At the same time, for those you perceive as dis-functional or non-functional, begin a discussion which attempts at the earliest opportunity to turn their position around and join the functionals. Find out why they currently think as they do, and then consider using the 'change equation' to explain why things will be better for them after the change has occurred.

   The **change equation** is expressed functionally as follows:

   $X < (A+B+C)$

   Where X = the cost of change to the team member;

   A = what's wrong with the present situation;

   B = the good things about the new scenario;

   C = the practical steps towards change that the team member must take.

Thus the totality of change is of greater benefit to the team members than simply staying put.

Case study

M, a team manager, wants to introduce new software which will enable specialist order processing to be done on the firm's computer system. Up until now it has been done manually. N, one of M's team members who is in charge of specialist order processing, argues that the current manual system does the job perfectly well and 'if it ain't broke, don't fix it'. M explains to N that the current procedure is slow, causes delayed delivery to the customer and has resulted in some paperwork loss and misfiling (A). Further, the speed, efficiency and reliability of the new IT based system will generate greater customer satisfaction and create the time and space to take on new business (B). Also, all you need to do, N, is to attend a half day session to show you how to use the very simple new software (C), since we will not be transferring existing manual orders onto the computerized system. Now isn't that a small price to pay for a much better way of doing things (X)?

It may be that the use of the change equation will have done the trick. Either way, you will know where you stand with that particular team member.

2. **Use specific tactics for each group**. So:
    - *Functionals*. All you may have to do here is pull sufficiently on the reigns so that these people in their enthusiasm can slow down and take stock for a moment, think through the consequences of the change, see more clearly the end result and focus their energies more precisely on the right route to follow. Do not, however, curb their enthusiasm. The functionals are your sales people for the other two groups, in particular the non-functionals. The drip, drip effect of your champions' zest may well be the ultimate turn around factor for the non-functionals.

- *Dis-functionals.* In some ways, the clear anti-change stance of this group is the easier of the two negative approaches to deal with. At least you know where you stand, and that gives you the ability to argue your case head to head against a counter-argument. Generate and keep open a dialogue with the dis-functionals. Hold regular meetings with them to keep them abreast of progress and continue the debate, especially to explain and sell them the successes so far and show how these counter their doubts. Use a reliable and solid team of functionals to support you in this. Eventually, most dis-functionals will grudgingly agree that the change appears to be for the better. If not, there are no doubt opportunities for them elsewhere!
- *Non-functionals.* Since these people will not face up to reality, it is difficult to create a strategy for dealing with them. Any effort you make will seem like trying to nail jelly to the ceiling. The longer term approach is the best bet here. Allocate a functional to each non-functional to take on a 'buddy' role. This way, the positive hand-holding approach of your supporter will gradually bring the non-functional around to face up to the change. By working with the functional on a day to day basis, the fears of the non-functional will dissipate as he sees the change beginning to work in reality.

3. **Monitor the progress of key influential team members.**

   You can do this by creating a *commitment chart*. This plots and monitors the current and desired positions of your more senior team members – the one best able to influence the more junior people for better or for worse. Here is an example of a commitment chart. The aim ultimately is to move everyone to the right hand side of the chart. Using this visual tool, you will be better able to identify those who can assist you in dragging the less committed towards your change goal.

Key people	Disfunctional (opposed)	Non-functional (laissez faire)	Semi functional (helpful)	Fully functional (make things happen)
A	O →	X		
B			X	← O
C		O →	→	X
etc				

For the purposes of this exercise, notice that the functionals have been divided into two streams to give you a little more flexibility in categorizing where people are. O is the current position; X is the next step desired position. Here are some points to note:

- The strategy for A, who is dis-functional, is to start by turning him into as non-functional. This may seem a rather strange approach until you remember that you are still dealing here with individuals, and, as a personality, A may be easier to handle as an ostrich than as a bear.
- B has backtracked. He was completely on board but now seems to have slipped a point or two and has nagging doubts. More reassurance work needs to be done with B
- C has been allocated a fully functional buddy, and your view is that this relationship will take C completely to the right in due course.

By using the commitment chart, you now have a clear view of where people are, the stages to take them through to get to the right and the amount of time and effort that you need to devote to getting them there.

Summary

Here is a summary of some practical tips and techniques to help you through change management:

- Assess whether change is being driven by internal or external factors. Your approach to managing the change will be different in each case. Consider whether a team driven or a leadership approach would work best.
- Avoid the key pitfalls which militate against successful change. In particular, don't be complacent, and remember to communicate every step of the way.
- Develop and use the key change leadership skills – the Change Leadership Dozen. For example, maintain a clear focus, use a solid structural process and generate support though constant communication with your team.
- Within any change procedures, ensure that you develop a strategy, put together a solid plan for its implementation and monitor progress every step of the way using GANTT or CORT charts. In a phrase, project manage the change process.
- Bring your people with you. Differentiate supporters from both active opponents and the ostriches, and manage each group towards a total team commitment to the new way of doing things.

TEN
Overcoming stress

10.1 I am finding life as a people manager tough because of everyday tensions brought about by the responsibilities surrounding constant human interaction with my team members. Sometimes I feel really stressed and almost unable to cope. Why is this?

There is no doubt that fresh responsibilities bring with them their own anxieties, and looking after a team of people is one of the most difficult jobs to handle. This is because human interaction necessarily involves the ups and downs of emotional input however hard you may try to avoid it. Before going any further, you can take heart from the fact that, like any other activity, things will become much more manageable as time goes on and your experience in handling people grows.

The first question to ask yourself is: do my feelings in this situation really make me feel over anxious and ill, or alternatively, although I feel tense, am I in fact getting a positive buzz out of my new role? This is not such a naive question as it may seem because there is good stress as well as **bad stress**. In fact, good stress is better described as **stimulating pressure**. The real negative stress is manifested when you are unable to cope through being overstretched to the point of irrational anxiety. It is also true that you can be stressed when you have too little to do (hence the saying 'boredom kills'). The relationship between these forms of stress/pressure looks like this:

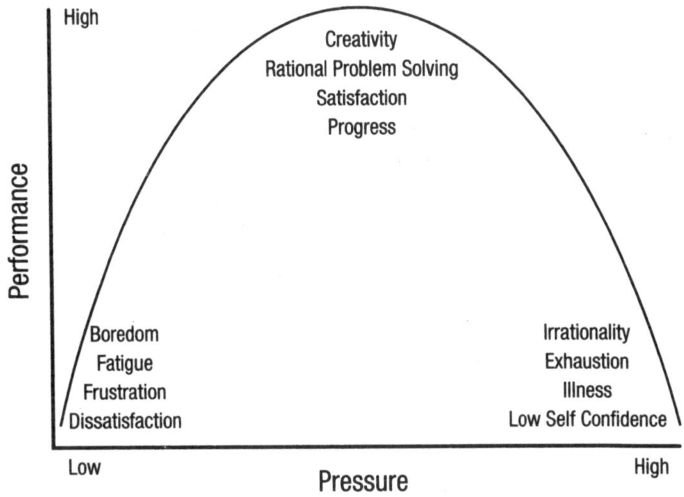

The Effect of Pressure on Performance

Thus, when the pressure on you is too high or too low, you become genuinely stressed; when the pressure is optimized at the top of the parabola, you achieve maximum performance by being positively stimulated by your work. This is how the same graph looks when considering your work behaviour in these situations:

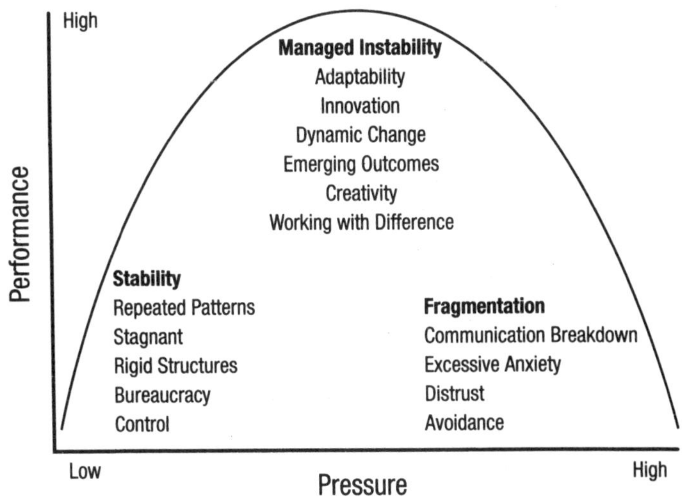

Work Behaviour Under Pressure

Let's concentrate now on the situation where the pressure on you is too high. You will assume here that excessive work problems are getting the better of you, but have you thought to question why it is that some colleagues appear to tolerate similar stress levels to your own with much more equanimity? There are two possible explanations for this:

The first is simply one of **personality**. Some people have an inherent capacity for absorbing and dealing with stress which is simply down to their tougher natural psychological make-up. There is little you can do about this except learn to handle stress better on the back of experience.

The second is based on an individual's personal history and how much **psychological baggage** you are carrying around subconsciously from events and experiences in your past. One way to understand this is to imagine your mind as a reservoir of water. What you must avoid is the reservoir overflowing. The reservoir, however, already has water in it generated by unresolved anxieties from the past. The amount of additional water that the reservoir can take from current anxieties about work (and possibly other external issues) will depend on how much of this pre-existing baggage is still around. Here is the reservoir in action:

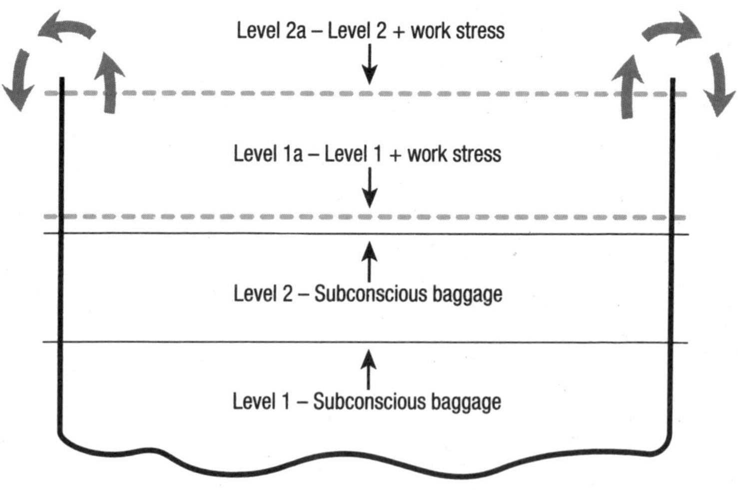

The Stress Reservoir

Thus, if you are a Level 1 person, the amount of stress you can cope with today at work will be more than if you are a Level 2 person. If you are a Level 2 person, you should seek immediate counselling to assist with lowering that pre-existing high level of subconscious baggage. This will enable you to begin to manage today's stressful issues in a much more focused and balanced manner.

10.2 What are the specific issues in my working life which are likely to be key stressors, and how can I resolve the resulting problems so as to reduce my stress levels?

There a number of general issues in our working lives which tend to be problematic and stressful. The illustration provides some examples generated both by the environment and also from within ourselves.

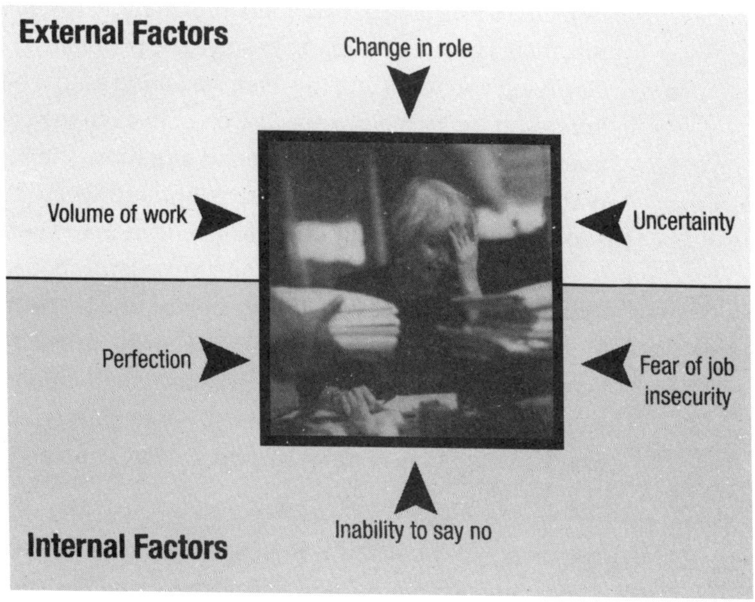

Causes of Stress

Here are some specific **examples of work related stress** and some suggested solutions for handling them effectively:

- *Confused and ineffective systems and procedures*. These are a recipe for chaos and stress. Either have a serious conversation with the powers that be to get things changed for the better, or, if it is a team issue, take the initiative yourself to improve the work processes that are causing the problem.
- *Excessively repetitious or monotonous work*. This arises at the low pressure end of the spectrum. As a people manager, you should now have the authority to spread the work around amongst team members including yourself, so that everyone is interested in and challenged by the variety of tasks with which your team is involved. If the problem lies with the projects your team are given, talk to your senior manager and ask for a more varied portfolio of matters to get involved with.
- *Uncertainty*. Uncertainty is caused by either a lack of clear objectives or a lack of cascaded information. In the former instance, you may be able to resolve the problem by simply clarifying your own and the team's position as to where you are going, or by nailing specific objectives to the carpet at your next appraisal. In the second situation, the fault lies with senior management. There is nothing worse that not knowing what is going on. It is senior management's job to ensure that you are aware of all the organization's issues that do or will affect you. If they do not, the rumours start to circulate and the resultant insecurity breeds stress. Scotch rumours by asking for clear and unambiguous information from your own manager. You are entitled to know whether the news is good or bad so that you can plan to take action accordingly.
- *Interpersonal conflict*. It is impossible to like everybody we work with. We all have different personalities, different values and different ways of approaching our work, and the human issues that arise as a result of these differences need

not and indeed cannot, for the sake of the business, result in hostility. Learn to work positively with everyone you come into contact with and use well developed communication and influencing skills to resolve problems and get things done without rancour. If there is a particular individual with whom you are experiencing significant difficulties, sit down with him for a heart to heart discussion and agree a sensible way forward for your working relationship. This includes the relationship with your direct manager where the problems often lie. Take the bull by the horns and sort things out – don't just live with it.

- *Inflexible and/or over demanding work schedules.* If this appears to be the case, begin by checking your self-organization systems to ensure that you are being as efficient as you can be. As part of this process, check your team's availability alongside your delegation strategy and ensure that you are maximizing the use of your human resources. If all this is satisfactory, go back to senior management and explain that the deadlines you are given or the resources you have at your disposal don't work in terms of executing a quality job. Be confident and assertive in doing this, be prepared for a negative response and, if the response is negative, be prepared to outline clearly the consequences of your lack of resources. If timescales come directly from clients, be clear about how long the job will take and make sure that the clients understand the reality of this. Remember that it is understood that we are all now seeking to experience a solid work/life balance. No one should be working uncontracted hours except by prior agreement, or via an understanding that work volumes fluctuate and that busy times are compensated for during slacker periods.
- *Presenteeism.* This is the attitude which suggests that you should always be around in the office, irrespective of whether your presence is necessary, because of outmoded views that if you are not in the building you are not

working. In other words, you are not trusted. It could take the form of standard 'clocking in and clocking out', or a need by your manager to see you around (an example of their insecurity), or the perception by your team that you should be the first in and the last out. You yourself can remedy this last example by educating your team on how all of you are expected to work most effectively to produce your target results. Some people, of course, have to be in the office – front room staff and those working with kit that can only be located in the office. But for the rest, dependant only on mobile technology, the office can often be the last place to be most productive. Remote working, with all the IT bells and whistles in place, allows managers the space to focus on important projects when necessary and is now becoming a normal part of working life. What is important to organizations in today's business world is not inputs but outputs. Those which insist on presenteeism and the stress it can cause have yet to grasp this profitable fact.

- *Lack of assertiveness*. The resolution of most of the above issues already discussed includes the need to state your views and express your opinions without fear or favour in a forthright and open manner. Why are you so afraid to do this? Why are you unable to say 'no'? You are doing a really good job, and because you can't refuse a request, more and more work demands are placed upon you – and the vicious circle begins.

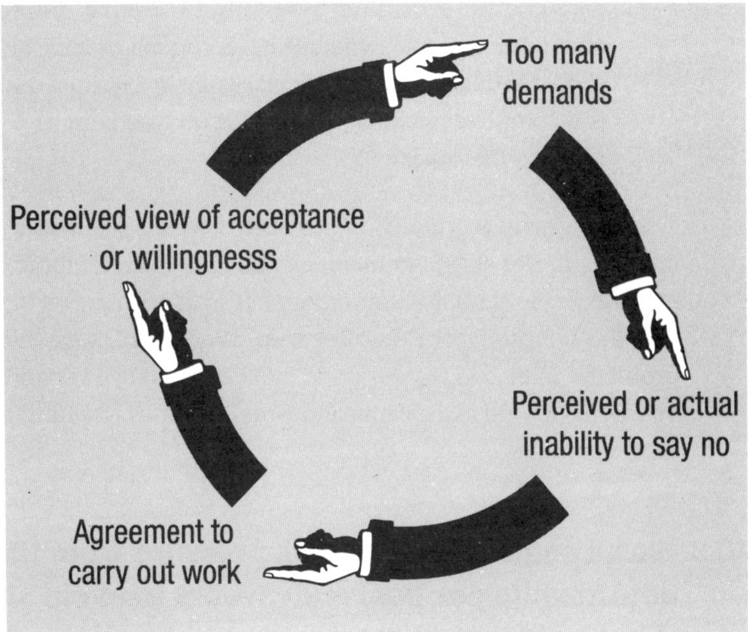

The Vicious Circle of Unassertiveness

What is the worst that can happen? You might be unfairly dismissed. If that happens, you are not only going to be compensated financially but will be delighted to be out of such an awful place to work. The more likely scenario is that you will be respected for putting across your thoughts and feelings on a particular issue, find that they are taken onto account when decisions are made and that your profile in your organization rises accordingly. Be confident in your interpersonal communication talents.

- *Work volume/perfectionism relationship*. Do you find it difficult to let a task go when you are not happy that the end result is perfect? If so, you will find that jobs take twice as long as they should, that your overall work load begins to pile up and that your stress levels rise proportionately through anxiety that you are not coping with your work volume. Fight this perfectionist obsession. Worrying for even a few seconds about, for example, whether it is a comma or a full stop that should be inserted at a particular point in a written document is a complete waste of time. Let it go – as long as it makes sense to the reader.

The response to this question has been directed at you as a people manager under stress. Remember that your team members could be suffering in the same sorts of way. If so, it is up to you to recognize the symptoms and to offer help. Where the stress-inducing problem can be laid at your door, make sure that you change your own behaviour to assist in making working life less fraught for your team members.

10.3 We all come under serious pressure from time to time despite our best endeavours to avoid stress. What personal strategies should be adopted to reduce the effects of stress to a minimum?

Here are some suggestions for keeping body and mind in one piece during the tough times:

1. **Objectives and values.** Are you clear about what you want from your life? Do you have a plan for taking your life forward? Have you a sense of what is important and what is not important to you? If your answer to any of these questions is 'no', take time out to think about these life issues until you can answer 'yes' to them all. The **L Map** below will give you a few pegs on which to hang your thoughts.

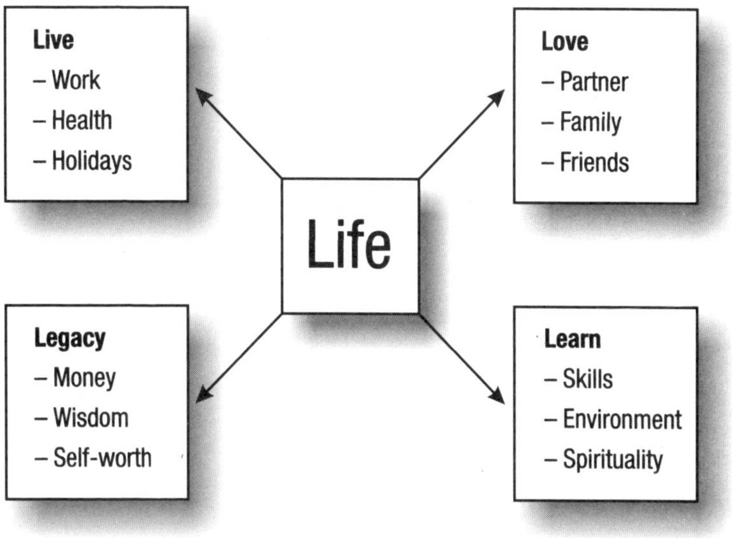

Life Map

The clarity that prioritizing through this exercise will bring to your life will make decision making easier, eradicate a myriad of anxieties and thus reduce your stress levels.

2. **Hobbies and other non-work interests.** Part of the work/life balance should include an activity in which you are seriously interested and in which you participate on a regular basis. It can be anything from quizzing to sport to model train building. The ability to focus and concentrate on something you enjoy outside your working environment takes away the mental strain which responsibilities at work necessarily produce.

3. **Exercise.** The old adage 'a healthy mind in a healthy body' is true. Choose a form of exercise with which your body feels comfortable. Not everybody needs tough work outs in the gym. This may be your interest, but others might consider swimming, jogging, walking, yoga, team games or even

regular gardening as their enjoyable form of toning up. Always do enough at least to feel your heart rate rising and the resulting warmth extending into the body's extremities, and do this three times a week.

4. **Sleep.** We tend to average about seven hours per night. Make sure you get that amount in order to recharge both your physical and mental batteries. And don't forget the post lunch nap which is now being touted by 'medics' in the know as seriously beneficial for us – although beware your business culture and likely response before trying this out!

5. **Diet.** This is not the place to discuss diet in depth. Suffice it to say that we are what we eat, therefore ensure that you have a balanced diet and take in the right amount of all necessary vitamins and minerals each day. Don't smoke, drink in moderation, limit caffeine intake, eat only one main meal a day and don't skip meals. Enough said!

6. **Develop and cherish personal support systems.** The security of having family and friends around us, particularly those we trust and know we can confide in, is vital to emotional well-being and stress reduction. Loneliness is psychologically damaging, and if you do not have family or a circle of close friends you can talk to in depth, develop such a network as soon as possible. This does not mean that you have to be with people all the time. Solitude is occasionally necessary for serious thinking. Just don't indulge in extended solitude which might well turn into loneliness.

Summary

Here is a summary of some practical tips and techniques to help you through a stressful period:

- Recognize the distinction between stress and pressure. Learn to revel in pressure but take counter measures to deal with stress. Assess your level in the stress reservoir.
- Identify the particular causes of stress at work and seek to counter them. Develop strategies to reduce the stress caused by particular problematic situations, and remember to assist your team members if they should be experiencing a difficult time.
- Create a work/life balance that works for you. Use external support to ease stress at work, and adopt a healthy and positive lifestyle.